How to Win

Profitable Business

Building Your Business
Other titles in this series are:

Know Your Law
by Greville Janner QC MP

How to Manage Money
by D Donleavy and M Metcalfe

How to Manage People
by Ron Johnson

For details see back of book

How to Win Profitable Business

Tom Cannon

Business Books

London Melbourne Sydney Auckland Johannesburg

Business Books Ltd
An imprint of the Hutchinson Publishing Group

17–21 Conway Street, London W1P 6JD

Hutchinson Group (Australia) Pty Ltd
30–32 Cremorne Street, Richmond South, Victoria 3121
PO Box 151, Broadway, New South Wales 2007

Hutchinson Group (NZ) Ltd
32–34 View Road, PO Box 40–086, Glenfield, Auckland 10

Hutchinson Group (SA) (Pty) Ltd
PO Box 337, Bergvlei 2012, South Africa

First published 1984
© Tom Cannon 1984

Set in Helvetica

Printed in Great Britain by The Anchor Press Ltd
and bound by Wm Brendon & Son Ltd
both of Tiptree, Essex

British Library Cataloguing in Publicatation Data

Cannon, Tom
How to win profitable business.
1. Marketing
I. Title
658.8   HF5415

ISBN 0 09 151840 7 (cased)
       0 09 151841 5 (paper)

Building Your Business

Series Editor: Tom Cannon

The last decade has witnessed a growing awareness of the importance of a healthy small business sector. The individuality, flexibility and creativity of the entrepreneur are recognized as vital to economic prosperity. Yet the same period has thrown up more and more challenges to the small firm. Competition has become more rigorous, while the need for efficiency and the effective application of resources has increased sharply. Perhaps the most valuable of these resources today is knowledge.

This series of books has been designed specifically for the entrepreneur, to bring to the owner and manager of the small firm vital areas of knowledge and information. The aim throughout has been to break down the barriers between theory and practice. The books are 'action-oriented' and this action-orientation is built into the texts themselves. Each book is broken down into self-contained Units. Each Unit sets out **Key Issues**, develops the issues and ends with **Action Guidelines**. Wherever possible, examples are drawn from the actual experience of small business people. Each author is an expert in his own field but equally at home with the application of his expertise to the small firm.

Growing recognition of the needs of the small firm has led to a range of initiatives to provide assistance. Government at a national and local level, large companies, banks and voluntary agencies are actively seeking ways to help the owner and manager of the small business to thrive. However the key characteristic of this type of company is its dependence on individual effort and skill. The onus for survival and prosperity lies on the man or woman who turns these ideas into action.

This series focuses on the key areas of customers, money, people and the law. The ideas presented will help provide the management expertise which leads to success.

Contents

Preface

This book is written for the entrepreneur, for the person seeking to shape his business and its future in the way most likely to ensure its effectiveness and profitability. If this description fits you, then the ideas, insights, techniques and approaches described here are designed for you. This is true whether you are:

- the prospective entrepreneur seriously considering starting up your own firm
- the owner of a very small concern, perhaps employing fewer than ten workers – including yourself
- the owner of the 'larger' small firm with anything between ten, and two hundred and ten employees
- the employed manager in either of these former concerns
- the manager of the small, operationally independent subsidiary of one of Britain's large corporations

As a sole trader, craftsman or managing director of a subsidiary of, say, Northern Engineering Industries, you will need to have other things in common if you are to get any real benefit from this book.

You will be:
- determined to make the best of your business and its opportunities
- willing to face the risks and challenges of growth either in terms of your own personal development or the company's
- open-minded enough to look outside yourself and the firm into the market-place for the main clues to the way your firm should go in terms of products, services and the diverse array of your offerings to the market

- creative enough to take the ideas presented here and, in the other areas identified, adapt them to your needs and turn them into positive action
- truly enterprising

You will not be:

- happy to potter along in an established routine unwilling to question its appropriateness for NOW
- convinced you know what's best not only for yourself but for your customers
- hostile to challenge or change
- frightened to invest now for returns in the future
- unwilling to plan, even if it means taking into account forces over which you have little control, such as changing conditions, competitive action and customer requirements

These personal features are the key to successful marketing. Small firms are about people. This and the ability of those running the business to stamp themselves on the firm which most clearly separates the small firm from the large corporation.

Much of the book emphasizes broad, generally usable ideas and notions. In specific contexts, the needs of special industries or types of firm are highlighted.

The sole trader, the partnership and the limited liability firm operate under different pressures. The back-up, the support and the resources available to the one, the twenty and the two hundred employee company have a direct impact on its marketing capability. The conditions, approaches and technologies available in different markets influence policy. The service firm, the manufacturer, the craftsman and the retailer, to name a few, each face specific circumstances, have particular resources to employ and have varied relations with their customers. These differences are part of the world of the businessman. They are central to this book.

When it comes to effectiveness in marketing, the well organized smaller firm has *all* the major advantages. It can use its short lines of communication, its close links with customers, its flexibility, responsiveness and creativity to build into all its operations an unbeatable marketing approach.

Inevitably a book like this is not the work of one man. Many others, notably the 400 plus small firms I've worked with over the last ten years, have been vital to the emergence of my ideas. My publishers have shown patience and forbearance. My wife, Fran, has borne the brunt of the hard work, while without Marianne Burnett, my secretary, it simply would not have appeared. Although these have played a part, the responsibility, should I say onus, for what is here lies with me, the author.

Tom Cannon

Section I

Marketing and Your Business

1
Marketing Today

- Marketing is a total approach to running a company and building a business.

- Marketing is as relevant and perhaps more vital to business in today's harsh economic climate as it was in the more buoyant sixties and early seventies.

- Marketing involves combining a variety of sometimes simple, occasionally complex, disciplines into effective managerial action.

- Marketing means looking outside the firm for the primary directions and basic responses to the challenges the company faces.

Introduction and Aims

The last few years have seen a growing awareness of the importance of marketing to the smaller firm seeking survival and prosperity. However, before we look at this, it is important to recognize that there is nothing new or revolutionary about challenge and adversity for the entrepreneur. Listening to some commentators, one would imagine that the entire history of business prior to 1974 consisted of days of wine and roses, with the possible exception of a half-understood and ill-recalled period called 'the 1930s'. In fact, winning profitable business has seldom been easy or automatic

The period since the mid-1970s has increased the challenges, but the underlying need for effectiveness is nothing new. Tough trading conditions mean that the businessman must add a new perspective to his business. **This is marketing**.

In this unit the intention is to:
- explore the true meaning of this vital concept
- highlight the many assets the small firm has in implementing the **reality** of marketing rather than merely the **appearance** of marketing
- bring out the importance of building this approach into all the firm's activities

An American experience

Supreme Furniture found out the importance of marketing when they first tried exporting their range of coffee tables to the United States. The firm had enjoyed good sales of these, notably nests of tables, in the UK for a number of years. The low value of the £ in the mid-1970s tempted them to seek sales in the United States. Armed with specially developed promotional material and 'very competitive' prices, and backed with considerable help from the BOTB, they spent almost £20,000 in sales, promotion and exhibition costs, but to no avail. Failure was total with only the recollection of the extravagant promises of a couple of import agents to sustain them.

Looking back, Sam Johnson, the owner and managing director, puts the cause of failure down firmly to their *product orientation*. His explanation goes as follows:

The nests of tables and coffee tables we make are a peculiarly British, perhaps European, product. They are designed to fit the needs of the typical UK lounge/living room. This is, in fact, a fairly small, rather cluttered area with a three-piece suite, hi-fi, television, wall unit, fire, hearth rug, even a tropical fish tank. This gives enormous advantages to a small, simple coffee table ideally fitting into a nest for easy storage. These are not truly working tables; at best they'll hold a cup, saucer and side plate.

In the United States the situation is very different. Lounge/living areas are much larger, with far fewer major items of furniture, perhaps a matching chair and armchair, hi-fi and television but probably no fire and far less clutter. Here, the smallness and ease of storage is no great advantage. At the same time, the table is expected to be far more functional. Meals will be eaten off it, not only the famous TV dinner, but take-aways and other fast foods. The size and style of our units were totally unsuitable:

❛ Our problem was that we were so obsessed with selling our product that, faced with the choice of either trying to change US housing styles, eating habits, expectations and values or changing our product, we in effect chose the former! ❜

Just what is marketing?

Supreme found that taking a marketing approach to prosperity meant re-examining their basic approach to their business. Sam thought in terms of the products they were making, how to produce them efficiently and well, and his internal operations. Unfortunately these cut no ice with new customers or middlemen. They buy because it is the right product (for them), available where and when they want it at the right price. Supreme's failure to recognize this and attempts to push an unacceptable product on an unwilling market cost them time and money. Efficiency and profitability are inseparable from good marketing. However, efficiency and profitability are based as much on understanding the the buyer as on understanding your own production.

The Institute of Marketing build this into their definition:

❛ Marketing is the management process which identifies, anticipates and supplies customer requirements efficiently and profitably. ❜

It is all too easy to be so involved in what the firm *is* making that we lose sight of what we *should* be making.

How can marketing help you?

The power of the marketing approach lies in bringing managers face to face with a number of simple lessons. The first of these is that the closer the firm comes to supplying customers with what they want, the more they will pay. The opposite is equally true. The further away it is from their ideal, the less they will pay.

Unfortunately it's not enough to just recognize this:

- Owners and managers must be willing to take action, to do something about meeting customer needs even if it is inconvenient, disruptive or 'not the way we've always done it'!
- They must look outside the firm for clues to what the customer wants. The more structured and systematic this search, the more likely the pay-off will be.
- It will generally involve some costs in time and money, if benefits are to emerge.

In turning these ideas to action, smaller firms have many assets. The in-depth knowledge of all facets of the firm and its operations, by top management, often means that there is a real feel for its true potential and ability to meet customer requirements. At the same time, their close contacts within the firm mean that once commitment at the top is established, it can readily be converted to managerial action.

In the minds of many small firm managers, there exists the notion that marketing means a lot of money and high, difficult-to-judge, risks. Most evidence points to the opposite conclusion; the reality of marketing is cheaper than the appearance.

It is often:

- the simple modification of a product.

Cameron-Price, a Birmingham based firm, adapted their moulded plastic footpump with 'a plastic tube, a filter, a small container and a face mask' to produce a simple compressor for asthmatic sufferers. The product was £10 versus the established electric air compressor's £100. Cameron-Price's hope is that it will double turnover within a year.

or

- a better combination of the existing price, promotion, distribution, service and product mix.

Lytham Marine achieved this when they restructured their boatbuilding operations. They found that the total cost of a new boat was deterring many potential buyers. In response, they introduced a DIY or, more accurately, finishing, scheme to their yard. They produced the hull and main features and rented space in their yard to individuals wanting to do the finishing work themselves. As part of the 'package' they gave advice, sold materials and if it all got too much, completed the vessel for the disillusioned. The result: a massive increase in through-put and profitability.

Although the breakthrough can lie in improving a single feature, as with Cameron-Price, more often it is through attention to the combination of features that success will emerge. This process is called managing the *Marketing Mix.*

The Marketing Mix is the combination of product, price, advertising and promotion, distribution and service that complete the 'total' package sought by the customer in the famous phrase: 'the right product, in the right place, at the right price!'

The key to success here lies in recognizing that all customers, industrial, government or private, seek a number of things when buying. They might need the product or service itself to complete a task or meet a need. However, no matter how good it is, if the customer is neither aware of its existence nor convinced of its value, it cannot succeed. The product or service has to be available in the way, place and form sought by the customer. Once these are combined, price will determine whether the customer can or will close the deal.

This is not true in commodity markets. Here, the customer views the products offered by all suppliers as exactly the same. There are no differences in service, reliability or quality between suppliers. The only RATIONAL criterion on which he can choose is price. The supplier has a choice. He can ignore the Marketing Mix and accept that his product is in a commodity market. The result — price competition; or he can develop the other variables, making the firm less vulnerable to price cutting. It is a company decision with the most dangerous situation facing the firm in the middle — no marketing effort and unable to compete on price.

Springfield Furniture found this out first with a setback, then with a success, in their exports. The firm supplied a wide range of furnishings to caravan manufacturers in Britain. Over a number of years a strong position had been established in the UK, but virtually no exports. The first move into exports involved the existing range of styles and designs at rock bottom prices.

Despite promises and near misses, no real headway was made. It soon became clear that the missing ingredient was effective representation. However, the specialized nature of their customer market meant that resolving this problem would not be easy. Agents with market knowledge were tied up. Those not tied up had no market knowledge.

They solved their problem with an ingenious tie-up with a German manufacturer of double glazing for caravans. A deal involving Springfield representing them in the UK and their representing Springfield in Germany, Holland and Belgium cracked the problem. Their new Marketing Mix opened up the market.

Little Boxes Once it is recognized that *business development, marketing* and *selling* involves bringing together the various strands of activity indicated above, it becomes clear that success lies in mobilizing all company resources.

Two comments illustrate this issue:

❝ In Britain the problem is not selling, but buying. ❞

❝ There are almost as many sales lost in the factory as are won on the road. ❞

The manager who quoted the second of these went on to say that a successful firm was one that maintained a profitable gap between the factory's losses and the salesman's successes.

Both highlight the importance of total company commitment to marketing. There is little point in the salesman winning a good, profitable new order if the despatch clerk sends the wrong or damaged goods. The restaurant which has a bright, attractive exterior but surly staff will soon be struggling.

Smallness is double-edged. Everyone can be committed to

building business and managing customer satisfaction. Management can reach everyone and should have sufficient understanding of their workforce to put the message across.

The little boxes which are often built up for protection against searching gaze or wider commitment can be broken down to the benefit of the entire firm. Customers assume greater and wider knowledge in small firms. They have specific expectations of the smaller firm in these areas.

A recurrent problem

The most common problem faced when a firm strives to introduce a marketing approach into its operations is turning ideas to action. The owner or chief executive might be fired with enthusiasm but, despite his encouragement, nothing happens. Often this is because the other managers or staff involved view this new idea as an implicit criticism or feel that new tasks are being imposed with inadequate additional help or resources. *A marketing approach can only be effective if the entire firm is committed.*

Resistance can only be overcome when:

- the issues which led to this development are openly discussed
- time is spent explaining and developing the ideas
- a coherent course of action is developed and probably backed by a plan
- adequate resources are made available
- top management commitment is clear

Marketing has little value to the smaller firm today unless it is converted into an operational discipline throughout the firm. The checklist which follows indicates some of the questions you should ask yourself when you seek to introduce this concept to your firm.

Action Guidelines _____

1 Are the chief executive and other senior staff willing to spend a significant proportion of their time on marketing?

Yes/No

_____
_____
_____

2 Is the firm willing to devote resources to the process of implementing marketing?

Yes/No

_____
_____
_____

3 Do management and staff spend time analysing individually *and* collectively customer views and attitudes to existing offerings?

Yes/No

_____
_____
_____

4 Has the firm recently introduced a major change in product or service based on identified and analysed customer attitudes?

Yes/No

_____
_____
_____

5 Do we know what business we are in?

Yes/No

_____
_____
_____

2
Building Marketing into the Firm

- Marketing is not something for one person or department. It involves the whole firm.
- Marketing means changing the entire outlook of the firm and organizing it to match this approach.
- Marketing orientated firms keep adapting and changing to keep in tune with the market-place.

Ask yourself why it was that:
- new firms like Apple revolutionized the small computer business?
- new companies like MacDonalds transformed fast food catering?
- Habitat, a new enterprise, created an upheaval in British furniture and furnishing retailing?

Instamatic cameras, photocopying, DIY retailing, leisurewear (blue jeans), catalogue shopping and double glazing. These are just a few examples of £ billion industries where existing firms in related areas were left standing while vast markets were carved out around them. The answer lies in the view of the world taken by established firms who were too busy with other issues to take the type of marketing approach needed to succeed in the new areas.

Introduction and Aims

The final question in the last unit: 'Do we know what business we are in?' is probably the most difficult and is certainly the most important question a firm trying to introduce and sustain a marketing approach will ever ask. It appears simple and most of us respond in terms of the products we make or the services supplied.
'I'm in the pen (or writing instruments) business.'
'I'm in the furniture business.'
'I'm in the rubber business.'
But, this is a *dangerous cul-de-sac.*

It is *dangerous* because a company survives or prospers in terms of its ability to match produce or supply with market demands, not in terms of an ability to make something.

It is *dangerous* because the firm's world is being defined narrowly in terms of particular production, manufacturing or service types or levels. This type of self-centred approach holds the seeds of the firm's greatest danger – self-satisfaction.

It is a *cul-de-sac* because thinking in terms of a particular product or service will ultimately lead to a dead end when the life cycle of that particular item is completed.

It is a *cul-de-sac* which restricts thinking about ways of meeting a market need, so that new developments or ways of satisfying customers are ignored. Established firms seldom successfully adapt to radical changes in their markets.

With developments as diverse as instant printing and Atari electronic games it is easier to describe the way the markets were built up after the event, than predict them. However, a pattern has emerged over the years. Firms which think of themselves and their customers primarily in terms of a product made or bought are vulnerable to new rivals. This is an easy trap with most of a manager's time and attention focused in one direction only. *Thinking in terms of customer needs and the benefits sought by the customer is the only sure way of avoiding that problem.* But the intangibility and complexity of these concepts makes business development in these terms very difficult for those used to calling a spade a spade, not 'a means of satisfying a movement or leisure need'!

In this unit it is intended to explore ways of understanding needs and making them more tangible. At the same time, approaches to reducing complexity will be studied so that firms can convert commitment in principle to management in action. Without this determination, it's a waste of time.

Here the smaller firm can hold most of the advantages – proper understanding by management of the firm's capabilities, ease of communication and freedom from bureaucracy. However such advantages are not automatically present in small firms. They simply cannot be matched by large firms.

Just what is a need?

In its simplest terms, a need is any lack, deficit or shortage felt by a person or organization. It is when the individual or firm seeks to satisfy these that it enters into commercial relationships. It is out of these that the business grows. They affect all business dealings from raw material supplier to manufacturer and assembler, wholesaler, retailer and end customer.

The true answer to: 'Do we know what business we are in?' cannot be arrived at until the firm can answer the supplementary issue: 'What need or needs are we satisfying?'

Here again the temptation is to respond in a product way; a need for rubber mouldings, or soft furnishings or toys. These are examples of how people or firms have satisfied needs, not the needs themselves.

Striving to achieve an understanding of his customers can be an uncomfortable process partly because the manager has to go outside the familiar surroundings of the product or service. Equally, this can be because most items or offerings can satisfy a variety of needs; sometimes a number of needs in a chain of supply. The answers are seldom obvious.

When talking of consumer products it can be useful to stand back and ask who buys it, when and why. Parker Pens gained an important insight into their operations some years ago from that simple process.

The first surprise was that the user seldom bought his own pen (in the more expensive ranges). The firm was already aware of the seasonality of their demand. Now it became clear that the vast bulk of their sales was by 'second parties' as gifts. Their conclusion: they were not in the pen market or the writing instruments market, but in the *gift market*.

This had an impact on virtually every facet of their operations from product development, through pricing and promotion to distribution. This last area vividly illustrates the impact of this concept. They extended their distribution far beyond stationers and traditional outlets to the largely unexploited gift and general goods network. In consumer products the link between seller and user is seldom a single step and often includes aspects ignored by suppliers.

In industrial markets there is often a greater consciousness that the buyer and the user are not the same. Despite that, it is unusual to find a small industrial supplier building into their marketing operations any explicit feature which acknowledges that the needs of the purchasing officer who places the order, the engineer who installs or specifies the line or the production manager who works with it, can be and normally are, very different.

In attempting to resolve this problem, the first step for a foundry in Glasgow was to draw up a diagram illustrating some of the characteristics in a 'typical' customer likely to have a significant influence on sourcing. Each then had certain needs identified with them. See Figure 1.

Careful analysis of their experiences established that in a number of their customers distinctive patterns could be identified.

The engineer's role was to give the technical specifications, identifying production tolerances. He frequently based his criteria on information obtained from his own firm's sales staff. They would be involved in choice of materials, finishes and general standards. In a new order situation the buyer's role could often be split into two parts. At an early stage he was mainly an information provider to the others. Later, with new projects, he put out the project to a short list of possible suppliers. Once the project was on-going their roles changed with, say, the engineer and the salesman taking a lesser part unless problems emerged. Perhaps more important, the foundry management found that:

(a) In different industries such as power supply and automotive, these relationships varied and effective selling had to adapt to them.

(b) The patterns changed over time with changes in personnel or order structure producing a marked effect on sales success.

There were two immediate pay-offs. *First*, a clear picture of the patterns of pressure and influence which determined choice emerged. This insight allowed the firm to spot pressure or influence points which could be exploited generally and with particular customers. *Second*, a realization that although 'typical' customers could not be identified, groupings of types emerged around whom special services could be built. For instance, the firms requiring high quality technical back up were separated from those seeking much more routine services.

Figure 1 *Customer characteristics*

Role	Need
Buyer	1 Minimum risk
	2 Ease of re-order
	3 Multiple sourcing
	4
Engineer	1 Efficient production
	2 Low maintenance
	3 Compatible with work practice
	4
Client's salesman	1 Customer acceptance
	2 Price saving opportunity
	3 Marketable advantage
	4

It's the firm not the man

As the picture builds up of needs, it soon becomes clear that

13

meeting them cannot be handed over to individuals or departments. Virtually every part of the firm is involved in matching its capabilities to customer requirements. Where this involves hard decisions, going against comfortable established practice, top management has to accept the responsibilities. For the foundry, realization that they were in the 'problem solving business' brought them face to face with the implications of solving problems.

For years the firm, in common with other foundries, had been under pressure to provide fully finished parts. They had resisted this because of the costs and responsibilities involved. However, once the step of recognizing their role as problem solvers emerged, the opportunity inherent in that step came into sharper focus.

Recognizing the true nature of the business they were in was only a first step in the process of becoming marketing orientated. It started influencing behaviour and performance as it was built into the thinking of virtually everyone in the firm. Top management had to accept responsibility for communicating the ideas, building them into their thinking and educating colleagues into this way of approaching the company's affairs.

There has to be a Marketing Champion in the firm. The *Marketing Champion* is a member of senior management with the time, energy and commitment to make sure that the new ideas are introduced, explained and followed through. A member of the top management team, ideally the chief executive, must be given specific responsibility for this. His/her task should be to prompt, search and promote awareness of customer needs and ways of servicing them throughout the firm. Dogged perseverance in the face of resistance is called for despite delays in getting immediate benefits. Without this, it will be too easy to revert to the comfort of an inward-looking product orientation.

Making it work

Although the entire firm has to be involved, specific responsibilities have to be allocated if commitment is to be converted to action.

The Marketing Champion cannot do it alone even if he thinks he can. He needs support both for his own sake and to ensure that an effective balance is built into company marketing operations.

Many firms make the mistake of believing that the appointment of a new marketing manager will solve the problem. Unfortunately, this is seldom the case. A small compression moulder in North Yorkshire found this to his cost. The initial commitment by the chief executive was there. A full time marketing manager was appointed. Sadly, staff in key areas such as sales and product development saw his role as threatening rather than creating opportunities. The marketing manager was increasingly isolated. The sales staff jealously guarded 'their' customers while pointing to the inability of the new man to make contact. The 'marketing' operation slowly degenerated into a fact-gathering operation with little apparent effect. The lag between identifying an avenue for development and measurable results can seem inordinately long to managers steeped in a tradition of fire fighting and crisis management. In this firm, before the ground work could pay off the new manager became disillusioned and left. A year later benefits were emerging from new industry customers but the drive had gone and new customers merely replaced declining accounts with no overall growth.

Three steps are necessary for these problems to be overcome:

1 *A Marketing Committee or Group* should be formed. It ought to involve a small but senior group of managers. Those involved in the critical decision areas of company direction, production, design, delivery and selling need to be represented. In very small firms these roles might be concentrated in only one or two people. Here some outsiders should be involved to provide alternative views on issues and routine around which policies can emerge

2 *Clear operational responsibilities* are needed for those directing the marketing effort. Access to top management, authority over sales development and scope to directly influence product and service policies, pricing and customer relations should be wedded to control of promotional and

---

distribution functions. Although ultimate responsibility here will lie with the chief executive, separate executive responsibilities are essential as soon as is practicable within resources.

3 *Some form of marketing planning* is called for. This will allow the more general direction the firm wishes to move into (its strategy) to be determined as well as the specific operations to achieve the strategy (the tactics) to be specified. The plan should be simple, short and jargon free.

Action Guidelines ━━━━━━━━━━

1 Identify key customers and customer groups.

_____
_____
_____
_____
_____
_____
_____
_____

2 Do the buyers buy for themselves or others? If others, how do they
   define items, services needed and sources of supply?

_____
_____
_____
_____

3 Describe in detail the process with all involved which leads to an
   order being placed.

   Step   *By Whom*   *Under what*
                                              Circumstances

   (1) Need identified _____   _____
                       _____   _____
                       _____   _____
                       _____   _____
                       _____   _____

4 Can any marketing pressure points in this process be identified?

                                            | Yes/No |

   If YES, specify_____

_____
_____
_____

5 Who are the key people in your firm, suppliers or customers able to influence these marketing pressure points or help you reach them?

(1) _____

(2) _____

(3) _____

(4) _____

6 How aware are these of the marketing goals you want them to contribute to achieving? (This should be related to frequency with which they are informed and their *stated* sense of involvement.)

_____

_____

_____

_____

7 Identify the need(s) met by your offering for the different groups who influence buying.

Influencer	*Need(s)*
_____	_____
_____	_____
_____	_____
_____	_____
_____	_____
_____	_____

8 Who is responsible for making sure that the firm's products or services effectively meet these needs?

_____

_____

9 Describe actions taken over the last two months to ensure this matching of needs and offering.

_____

_____

_____

_____

3

Marketing Has to be Managed

- **Many small firms have poorer marketing controls than large firms.**
- **Marketing consists of clearly defined objectives and actions to improve the firm's competitive position.**
- **Efficient management brings controls, objectives and actions together to increase profits.**

Introduction and aims

Perhaps the most dangerous and misleading comment ever made about a marketing activity states:

❝ I know that half my advertising works, but I don't know which half. ❞

This implies a level of inefficiency and lack of control alien to a good manager. Here, the aim is to establish the framework within which efficiency can be improved and effective controls emerge.

There are two interlocking elements in successful marketing management.

1 A consistent policy of building up an understanding of the customer and his needs. The more successful the match between product or service and need, the lower the investment in sales and other costs to bridge any gaps.

2 A management stucture forcing people to look outside themselves and the firm.

The two elements are brought together through a programme of continual learning and adaption.

19

The key features in this process are highlighted here. The importance of clear objectives plus methods of assessing the firm's progress towards them cannot be understated. These are often linked with targets and standards of practice or operations. Everyone affected should be involved in this process. The greater the sense of identity with any objective the higher the probability that it will be achieved.

Objectives and controls

The heart of any system of marketing control lies in a clear, coherent and well laid out approach which links the goals, objectives or aims of the marketing effort to the internal systems established to achieve them. The greater the mismatch between purpose and system, the worse the results.

As a minimum commitment, a firm which intends to achieve marketing objectives needs to *state* them clearly. These are not simple reiterations of vague company goals but specifically related to the precise markets the firm wants to reach. Precision is critical. Ambiguous or poorly defined goals are little better than no goals.

Problems here are depressingly common. In marketing, two misleading forms occur which can be summarized as:

❛ *Draw Your Own Conclusions* ❜

❛ *Better, Better than Something* ❜

Draw Your Own Conclusions This mixes detailed, apparently specific, analyses of the firm's position with largely untestable random assertions about customers or the market. Such an approach to objective setting is not properly structured and only contains a welter of separate points with few clear links. Goals are seldom stated. The staff expected to contribute to their achievement are left either to infer the objectives or simply to implement related strategies.

The operational result is often confusion and misdirected effort. The lack of clarity can mean that different, even conflicting initiatives can be taken at various times and in separate parts of the firm. Such a statement reflects either an unwillingness to be decisive or a fear of the commitment and responsibility inherent in a decision.

Better, Better than Something   This form of setting goals usually means seeking simple improvements on previous performance – improve sales, increase profitability, etc. These are seldom specific, often taking no notice of changing circumstances or new opportunities. Across-the-board increases in sales other than the unreal effects of inflation are rarely possible. Failure in these circumstances is easily excused by 'new' or 'changed' market conditions. Frequently these could have been predicted by rigorous analysis of market conditions.

Marketing objectives should be:
- **Clearly and simply stated with ambiguities avoided**
- **Actionable within the resources and time-scale envisaged**
- **Communicable in a way which leaves no-one in doubt about their meaning and his or her role in this process**
- **Internally consistent to ensure that they move the firm forward positively and consistently**
- **Quantified where possible**

Few firms can handle more than four or five objectives in a satisfactory way. Too many goals usually mean either lack of rigour or confusion between objectives and policies. The former is a statement of the position the firm wants to reach, the latter its way of getting there.

Objectives are the solid core around which marketing management build the operations. They provide the lead into effective strategies, policies and controls. They should be just as familiar to all staff involved in their achievement as operating instructions are to technical staff.

Performance, benchmarks and budgets

An effective system of objective setting and controls will ultimately mean that the manager can gauge with increasing precision the returns and impact of his efforts. It follows that monitoring performance should be an everyday part of the top manager's job. This will be in terms of two interrelated sets of criteria – the objectives themselves and certain specific key criteria.

These performance criteria include:

- *Market Share*   Many small firms argue that their overall share is too small for measurement to be meaningful. This may reflect too wide a definition of its market. Once the company's true market has been identified and its share and that of its competitors assessed, a sound basis has been established. A company without a clear idea of its share cannot have a clear idea of its performance.

- *Account Mix*   This incorporates two features of performance. These are the actual mix of accounts, large/small, local/national, etc., and the extent to which these match the performance of key competitors.

- *Marketing expenditure to Sales Ratios*   Careful monitoring of this will not only highlight any sharp hiccups or problems but can give a historic record against which future budgets, even achievements, can be measured.

- *Customer profiles and opinions*   Ultimately these will be the primary determinants of performance. The customer profile is particularly important for smaller firms as apparent stability may mask dramatic changes. A company might be supplying a sector of the distributive network, e.g. wholesalers, whose overall share of trade is falling rapidly. Even if this is not yet affecting sales, it will do so eventually.

  Customer opinions are often known in a general way, but details are frequently held only in certain quarters. A programme of bringing this intelligence together can highlight issues before they affect performance.

Much of this has emphasized the importance of establishing patterns and pictures. The chore of gathering these together and organizing them into a meaningful profile is generally rejected by management of small firms. Tragically this can mean that hard lessons have to be learned repeatedly, sometimes with fatal results for the firm.

Establishing *benchmarks for performance* is a simple way of minimizing the time and cost of this process. Some will be time-related with the previous impact of a given activity being the basis for judging performance. Others will mean taking into account cyclical and seasonal forces in the market-place. The greater the operational familiarity with these benchmarks, the easier fine tuning becomes. This can be geared to improve effectiveness or cut costs if problems emerge.

Any scientist or engineer will confirm that it is the accumulation of data and the testing of experiments and machines against the data that lead to progress. This is equally true of managing marketing.

Budgeting is inseparable from this process of setting and achieving objectives. Unless funds are provided, goals cannot be met. Conversely, unless the firm has established a clear sense of direction, the monies will be inefficiently expended, even wasted.

The progressive accumulation of knowledge about the firm, its market and the relationship between these is a critical element in setting marketing budgets. Within these guidelines the key to budgeting is linking budgets to objectives.

The temptation to:

- base budgets on previous years' expenditure
- think in terms of a fixed percentage of costs, for sales costs
- seek to match in some way competitive expenditure
- avoid establishing any budget, as 'money will be available'

should be avoided.

In the real world neither budgets nor objectives exist in a vacuum. Objectives for fish farmers might include:

1 establishing farmed trout and salmon in X per cent larger supermarkets and store groups

2 creating a high level of awareness of the low and reducing price of farmed products among customers, particularly the younger age groups on social classes B, C_1 and C_2.

However, these national objectives may be simply unachievable within the resources available to the industry. Some of the most cost-effective national media may be unusable because of the high initial costs. Two alternatives are open – to increase budgets dramatically or to establish realizable objectives. In this case, it may be decided to concentrate efforts in a particularly appropriate area. A successful initiative might then lead to additional resources being generated for future investment.

Throughout this programme of activity the key to long-term success lies in seeking improvements in marketing productivity.

Using the approaches identified above, budgets for contacting new customers, building up awareness of uses among established customers, and increasing market share, at the expense of particular rivals, can be established. Relating costs, hence budgets, to aims is central to effective marketing management.

Resources and opportunities

So far, considerable emphasis has been placed on the aspects of marketing activity or resources at the firm's disposal. The ability of the owner/manager or proprietor of the smaller firm to mobilize fully and effectively company capabilities to achieve its objectives provides the key to the operational strength of his firm. In larger firms, bureaucracies, procedures or simply size make this very difficult to achieve. However the manager must understand these capabilities both separately and as a whole.

The company presents to *any* prospective customer a total offering. This goes beyond the physical product or service to its availability, reputation and price. *Benefits based on the combination or mix of these provide the buyer with the satisfaction he seeks.* The term commonly used to describe this is **the**

marketing mix. In general, managers should avoid thinking in terms of the separate parts, for example sales force actions or improved delivery, other than in purely operational terms. It is the total effect which determines the pattern of demand.

Managing marketing means recognizing the varied and complex nature of the demand patterns facing the firm. Over-wide generalizations about trading conditions can lead to poor solutions. This can occur under generally favourable conditions where weaknesses in certain areas are ignored.

A Birmingham based clothing company found this a few years ago. Strong sales in a few areas were disguising the virtual extinction of key ranges.

Equally, overall response to poor overall trade can lead to missed opportunities for profits and pay-offs.

A plastics company in the South Midlands had been cutting prices overall to keep sales up. However, for certain products demand was not sensitive to price. Fairly radical increases dramatically improved profits, but sales were stable.

Few markets face wholly stable trading conditions. Sales can be influenced by seasons, fashions, changing tastes. The salient features of demand need to be fully understood and closely watched. One way of doing this is in terms of Demand States.

Figure 2 *Demand and the tasks of marketing management*

Demand state	Underlying customer attitude	Task
Negative	Hostility	Overcome dislike
Nil	Indifference	Stimulate
Latent	Unsatisfied need	Inform and develop
Faltering	Declining interest	Revitalize
Irregular	Intermittent requirement	Synchronize
Full	Desire	Maintain
Overfull	Excessive desire	Control

Source: adapted from P. Kotler, *The Major Tasks of Marketing Management.*

25

The manager should look at his products and their target markets in terms of these demand states.

A manufacturer of plastic rain barrels found demand was highly seasonal. Virtually all his sales came in the period March/July. His capacity out of this period, particularly September/November, was seriously underutilized. He decided to overcome this 'irregular' demand by a modified new product using his capactiy – children's 'Play-Barrels'. His sales for these were largely during the pre-Christmas period September/November.

The marketing orientated manager must look beyond the narrow bounds of his own product or service. A 'Substitutability Index' is very useful. The company looks at rivals and their products or services. These should be defined fairly broadly. He weighs them in terms of their ability to replace/be replaced. Thus a silicone rubber firm might give a locally based competitive product of silicone rubber a weighting of 10 but a national asbestos manufacturer perhaps 7. These change over time but can be invaluable clues for current action and future development.

To sum up

Successful approaches to managing marketing are built on a mixture of appropriate frameworks and accumulated knowledge.

The concepts introduced here, notably:
- The importance of objectives
- The system of management control
- The criteria against which performance is judged, allied to a commitment to accumulate, structure, learn from and adapt to the lessons of experience, can play an important part in wedding theory and practice.

In any smaller firm the greatest pay-offs will emerge from this process if others are involved in it. The potential returns will be reduced if the chief executive tries to go it alone. The objectives most likely to be achieved are those agreed to. It is surprising how demanding staff will become of themselves, given the chance. Eventually all these activities must take place within an appropriate organizational structure.

Action Guidelines _____

1 State the firm's four or five major marketing objectives. Indicate whether they are: actionable, unambiguous, communicable, internally consistent and quantified.

Actionable   Unambiguous   Communicable   Internally consistent   Quantified

i _____

ii _____

iii _____

iv _____

v _____

2 Faced with the same statements, who else has agreed with your evaluations?

_____

_____

_____

3 Describe the steps taken to communicate these objectives to those responsible for their implementation.

i _____

ii _____

iii _____

4 What actions are adopted to assess awareness of objectives?

_____

_____

_____

_____

5 State the firm's market shares in:

	%	%
Primary market(s)	_____	_____
Secondary market(s)	_____	_____

6 Indicate the company's mix of accounts:

(a) Large versus small (%) _____ v _____

(b) Local against national (%) _____ v _____

(c) New and old (%) _____ v _____

(d) Manufacturing or service (%) _____ v _____

(e) Any other category (%) _____ v _____

7 Marketing expenditure to sales ratio

(i) Last full year

(ii) Previous year

(iii) Previous year

8 Customer Audit: indicate major customers (actual, previous and potential), buyers and key to their business.

	firm	buyer	value (£)	key to business
Actual				
(a)	_____	_____	_____	_____
(b)	_____	_____	_____	_____
(c)	_____	_____	_____	_____
(d)	_____	_____	_____	_____
(e)	_____	_____	_____	_____
Others	_____	_____	_____	_____

29

Previous

(f) _____ _____ _____ _____

(g) _____ _____ _____ _____

(h) _____ _____ _____ _____

Others _____ _____ _____ _____

Potential _____ _____ _____ _____

(i) _____ _____ _____ _____

(j) _____ _____ _____ _____

(k) _____ _____ _____ _____

Others _____ _____ _____ _____

9 What is the total marketing budget for the firm's activities over the next year?

_____

_____

_____

How can this be allocated in terms of:

(a) functional costs? _____

(b) natural costs? (state areas) _____

(c) fixed? _____

(d) variable? _____

(e) direct? _____

(f) indirect? _____

10 What is/are the demand state(s) facing the firm?

_____

_____

_____

_____

11 How does the organization of the firm's operations reflect this?

_____

_____

_____

4

Organizing Your Marketing

- Success means building the basic approach into *all* the firm's operations.
- Effectiveness requires thorough understanding of the requirements of all parts of the firm.
- Efficiency is based on careful design of the structure and pattern of activities.

East Kirkby Carpets have been carpet manufacturers since 1947. The present Managing Director is the son of the founder and although it has been a public company since 1964, the family influence remains strong. The bulk of its production is medium/high quality Axminsters at its East Kirkby site which is near Liverpool.

Export organization

The proximity to Liverpool has played a part in encouraging the firm to build up its exports. These are primarily through agents working on a percentage basis. This policy has enabled the firm to build up a very extensive network of national agents throughout the world.

Traditionally the white Commonwealth has been their largest market with Canada and Australia the leading markets. Recently there has been some decline in sales to both countries with import restrictions making trade difficult to build up. However, the growth of demand in Europe, the USA and the OPEC has more than compensated for the decline in traditional markets.

The oil price rises and comments about the oil rich Arab states has prompted the initiative in the Middle East. Two basic approaches had been taken:

- working through contractors in the UK, particularly those involved in major building projects
- building up a network of agents.

A number of relatively small orders have been won.

The current sales set-up is based on Mr D. Smith as Sales Director and Export Sales Manager and is organized on a regional basis:

Figure 3   *Current sales set-up*

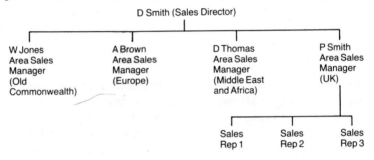

Mr D. Smith takes personal responsibility for the contracts side of the business and developing markets. In 1978 there was growing disquiet in the firm about poor returns from exports. Analysis of sales indicated the pattern shown below.

Figure 4   *Markets as a share of Kirkby Carpets' business*

Country	1970 %	1974 %	1975 %	1976 %
UK	80	74	70	70
Australia	7	6	5	4
Canada	5	3	3	2
New Zealand	2	2	2	2
Sweden	1	1	2	2

Switzerland	–	1	3	1
Germany	–	1	2	3
South Africa	2	1	–	1
Eire	2	–	–	1
USA	–	2	2	4
Netherlands	–	–	–	1
Iran	–	2	–	1
Saudi Arabia	–	1	3	2
Nigeria	1	1	1	1
Other Commonwealth	–	1	3	1
Other Europe	–	1	3	2
Other OPEC	–	2	1	1
Others	–	1	1	1
Total	100	100	100	100

This clearly demonstrated a mismatch between the sales set-up and current sales. The structure reflects a past situation.

Aims and objectives

A recent book on marketing described a 'relatively small' Swiss company which had over twenty staff in its marketing department. For the overwhelming majority of small firms many of the tasks identified with specific managers in this company – sales, marketing research, design, advertising, pricing and distribution – have to be done by one or a very small number of people.

The basic jobs of customer relations, pricing and spending in areas such as advertising are often seen as so critical that most chief executives are loath to delegate or pass on responsibility. This can lead to operational inefficiency and demotivation of those charged with implementation. A small firm must face up to the challenge of wedding the necessary commitment of the chief executive to the need to build the marketing approach into all facets of the firm but within the resource constraints faced by such firms.

Organizational structures exist to perform the tasks, current and future, laid down by the firm or its owner, in the most effective way. However, most small firms do not plan their marketing organization, often assuming that any pattern is adequate as long as attitudes or people are right. This can be fatal, particularly when the firm's shape becomes frozen in a specific approach.

Institutional deep freeze

Many factors contribute to this inclination towards *institutional deep freeze*. The most common in small firms is probably the reluctance to disturb personal relations and habits until the crisis is too grave to be avoided (or resolved). In marketing this often shows itself when the dominant approach has been selling.

> In a medium sized Midlands vehicle company, the sales director had always led the firm's business development effort. His skills in selling, sales management and customer liaison were unmatched. However, as the need for strategic thinking, market development and effective management of the marketing mix grew in the fiercely competitive environment of the early 1980s, his limitations became increasingly obvious. Despite this and serious sales decline, top management was very reluctant to take any action because of historical and personal factors. Inevitably the cure, when eventually taken, was harsh on both the company and the man.

Unless positive action is taken early, organization and behaviour will be like those in East Kirkby, determined primarily by previous events and experiences rather than future aims or expectations. The better the match, the greater the efficiency and the less likely waste and high costs. Much of this section will be addressed to converting this notion into action.

Probably the most common response to questions about marketing organization and structure is to pull out the 'organizational chart'. The smaller the firm, the greater its irrelevance, but the more likely this chart will be used for formal descriptions. The typical organizational chart with its neat little boxes, straight lines and comfortable job titles is generally irrelevant to marketing in small firms. It suggests a rigidity which is almost counter-productive. A systems approach with its interdependencies and blurred boundaries is far more useful.

Figure 5, suggests the nice, neat lines and relationships that do not reflect reality. In most cases it is more important to think how people will work together than recognizing who is top dog. Figure

6 provides a more useful procedure for this, mapping relationships and highlighting the extent and role of any overlaps that exist. Too often in organizational design the desire to describe hierarchies dominates the need to perform tasks.

Figure 5   *Organizational chart 1*

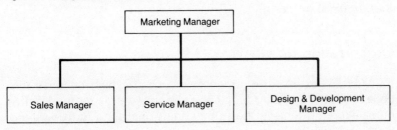

Figure 6   *Organizational chart 2*

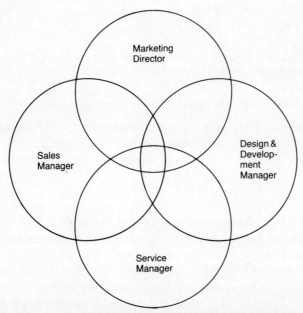

The specifics of marketing organizational design must be examined and, at the same time, note must be taken of the changing nature of marketing. Major trends ought to be built into this pattern. A clear illustration of this is the growing importance of service and services.

Support services, ranging from computer aided design to stockholding and technical back-up, are increasingly important in winning and holding on to business. The central importance of the service sector is seldom acknowledged. The vast bulk of smaller firms are in services or retailing. The appropriate form of marketing organization for this type of enterprise may be very different from that in manufacturing.

Organization for what?

Individuals set up firms or operate through them because they believe that organizing themselves in this way is more effective, more likely to achieve their goals than operating individually or through some loose association.

- **The aim is clear – we organize to win.**

The structure adopted must therefore be designed to provide competitive advantage. Any form of marketing operation must be geared to prompt a clear 'YES' to the question 'Does it confer a competitive advantage (or at least avoid disadvantage)?'

The approach adopted should be measured against the **industry success factors**, those issues peculiar to both the firm's and its customers' industry which appear closely associated with success.

A small Newcastle based data processor identified three **industry success factors**. The first of these was *customer intelligence* sufficiently exact to identify the type of user, large enough to be worth dealing with but not so large as to have in-house facilities. The second was *guaranteed rapid turn-round*. The closer the company came to a guaranteed 24-hour turn-round without massive spare capacity, the greater the likelihood of success. The third was *reputation for quality and security*. The more confident clients were in these, the greater the likelihood of good quality repeat business.

Building the operational structure around these key activities is more likely to confer competitive advantage on the firm than any conventional structure. Small retailers often slip into the trap of establishing their administration around inappropriate models. Diagnosis of the firm's internal organization and external needs should lead to some basic points around which the framework can be built.

Besides these, the marketing organization must satisfy two further conditions.

1 It must run itself as a functional area of the firm.

2 It must provide positive and supportive links with other parts of the firm.

❮ New organizational designs must reflect the post-industrial values. The designs should include full and free communication, regardless of rank; power consensus rather than coercion or compromise; and influence based on technical competence and knowledge rather than whims or prerogative of power. ❯

Most small firm managers, particularly those who have started their own businesses, would warm to these sentiments. Many have set up their firms to break free from the barriers described above. Despite that, it is very easy to slip into this mode of operation. An open, flexible, creative and responsive organization will not emerge by accident. In determining the base approach, three broad alternatives predominate:

Functional organization
Product based organization
Market orientated organization

Functional organization

This emphasizes the specific areas of marketing activity: advertising, selling, design, market research, etc. These are the cost and activity centres most easily identified with jobs to be done and related expertise. Unfortunately, in a number of situations commonly found in smaller firms this solution is far from ideal.

Difficulties Where the firm has a number of products or services and/or range of different customer types or markets, difficulties can rapidly emerge with resource allocation and the attention given to the varied situations faced. Firms in services or distribution (for example wholesalers and retailers) seldom find that these conventional structures highlight the key areas of their activities. In retailing, the role of 'middleman' demands a process perspective at the centre of operations, that is the ability to look back to suppliers and forward to customers simultaneously. A final difficulty with this approach has emerged over the last decade. Success in building business is increasingly determined by areas of activity not traditionally seen as part of their preserve – credit management, order processing, distribution, etc. Attempts to assimilate these into functional structures can lead to a proliferation of new functions, further bureaucracy and a great deal of operational overlap.

The apparent logicality and simplicity of this approach can be appealing, **but it is seldom if ever the best approach for smaller firms.**

Product based organization

Many companies with a wide range of products, brands or services have developed product based organizations. These structures are based on the firms' different offerings. Each is treated as a separate smaller firm or operation. It can be a discrete profit centre despite its shared production or distribution system. Individuals in the company are given separate responsibilities for the different offerings if this is to work, for example manager X is primarily responsible for product A. This means that he can champion it within the firm while balancing its various functional marketing inputs into a complete effort.

Difficulties   However, this approach can be very expensive to run, particularly if the link between increasing sales and profits is not direct. This organizational structure is strong in building volume, but at a cost. Where there is real scope for sales loading – high volume, low profits – the costs can be considerble. At its best it can capitalize on individual enterprise, but sometimes this enterprise can be lacking or need support.

38

Systems of triangular team building can be very effective in smaller firms large enough to allocate operations around separate products or services. The following diagram (Y) (see Figure 7) describes a plastics firm with 170 employees which successfully restructured its activities in this way. The owner is at the hub of the operations which are split into three distinct areas:

Manager A looks after garden and DIY products. These are primarily the firm's own lines sold direct to wholesalers and retailers. Advertising, display discounting and the talent to come up with new product ideas are vital here.

Manager B is in charge of catering and food processing products. Although these include a wide range of own lines, these are normally adapted to suit particular large clients. These are major food, catering or processing firms.

Manager C is involved in an array of custom made products usually made to customer specifications. His and his staff's technical problem solving ability is critical to success.

Figure 7 *Y diagram*

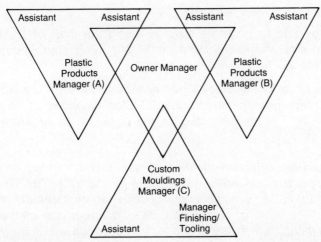

The importance of the service sector in any discussion of smaller firms, allied to the significance of the service dimension in much small firm customer/business development, makes product or service based organization difficult to convert to action. At the same time, many owner managers find it hard to give their product/service managers the operational discretion required if this approach is to be effective.

Market orientated organization

In all likelihood the organizational structure most able to generate the best returns to a small firm will be MARKET based. Most small firms handle a diverse array of different markets or customer types. A market centred structure uses these as the points around which the structure is built. This enables the company to get the best from the limited resources it can invest in particular areas, while ensuring that it provides a consistent and coherent image to customers.

The company's ability to define the markets in a way providing the best results will improve over time.

The company might follow the approach of a Coventry based plastic pipe producer, which divided its trade into consumer, industrial and local authority.

It is possible to be more specific along the lines of the North Eastern steel stockholder. He identified mining, shipbuilding and construction.

A timber firm in the Black Country took this a step forward. This firm noted the Standard Industrial Classifications of its major customers. These were used as the basis for its organizational structure.

Standard industrial classification   This provides the basis on which industry is sub-divided by government for statistics. The Minimum List Heading (MLH) is the category under which particular sectors fall and are used for government data collection. Hence the MLH for the paint industry is 274 and for iron castings is 313. Aggregate data on such key issues as imports, exports, production and numbers of employees is published regularly. Careful use and analysis can highlight both overall trends and key issues. Market research firms such as 'Market Location Limited' have used this for detailed further analysis of regional and corporate performance.

Black Country Timber found that their turnover was based on:

Customer industry	MLH	Share %
Agriculture and horticulture	001	30
Coal mining	101	25
Other mining, quarrying and extraction	102 103 109	15
Furniture	457	20
Others		10

The firm found that these industries had special characteristics which require specific approaches.
Organizing the sales team along these lines helped to ensure that they met the special needs of these industries.

Although these illustrations are mainly manufacturing orientated, some of the most successful and profitable uses of this have been in distribution and services. The steel stockholder just mentioned illustrates the way a distributor can employ this method.

A small London based design firm clustered its marketing activities around the educational, retail and leisure markets.

None of the firms described above employed more than ninety people. The number of managers involved was small but their expertise in their markets enabled them to develop a structure capable of getting the best returns.

People

Recruiting, managing, motivating and controlling those who make up the firm's marketing organization pose recurrent problems for managers of smaller firms. The difficulties go beyond the normal run of managerial/staff appointments, since many entrepreneurs are dealing with new areas of activity where the gap between action and response can be long and complex.

Numerous managers recount tales of the problems created by their first marketing appointment. Sometimes these emerge from a failure to recruit the right individual. Occasionally the role (threat) of marketing is misunderstood. Periodically marketing efforts are misapplied. Careful preparation and planning are needed to set up an effective marketing organization.

Some use of outside expertise will pay massive dividends in areas such as designing job descriptions and selecting the right, key personnel.

Beyond these, two factors are essential to success:
- Access by marketing staff to the chief executive
- Clear understanding of the role and position of marketing **throughout** the firm.

The second of these poses recurrent difficulties. A balance has to be established between giving marketing an exaggerated role and creating resentment, and turning it into a neglected backwater. Both are real possibilities, especially when new staff are involved. Marketing staff must work in particularly good harmony with sales staff, recognizing their mutual interdependence. Unfortunately, this is seldom achieved easily.

Education and training of all related staff is critical if their potential is to be achieved. This will mean a significant customer orientated role. Under no circumstances should sales staff be permitted to block access to customers.

An engineering firm in Wales gained little value from marketing staff, as the sales director blocked the route to an effective business development role. By relegating the new manager's role to preliminary investigation of opportunities, market research and public relations, he prevented any meaningful customer links.

This sales director had been so poorly briefed that he feared and resented the introduction of a function capable of dramatically improving his performance.

Links with other areas

Marketing is a relatively new area for many managers. Often it will be introduced as a new discipline or approach to their operations, perhaps to boost performance. This may be done to prompt change in a number of parts of the company. This is seldom welcomed by those with established systems and ways of working.

At the same time, marketing is change and adaption orientated. The entire philosophy underpinning it is geared to moulding or shaping the firm and its activities around the market. This often causes necessary dislocation and disruption in other parts of the firm.

Marketing staff often seek goals and perform tasks in ways which do not sit easily with the aims and functions of other departments or comfortable routines. Managing these tensions and potential conflicts is critical to the success of a marketing orientated firm. For some, the solution is simple – marketing dominates – with the chief executive fully identified with this conclusion. More frequently the answer lies in managing conflicts in ways which ensure that the benefits of competition are earned without paying the price of discord. Understanding the different potential 'flash points' will help you to achieve this. (See Figure 8.) Although the list which follows indicates some of the flash points, inevitably these are generalized and should be adapted to particular circumstances. This is particularly true of retailers and service companies where different pressures exist, for instance standardization versus bespoke, and alternative forms emerge.

Figure 8   *Marketing and other activities – flash points*

Activity/department	Their emphasis	Marketing's emphasis
Research and development	Basic research	⚡ Applied research
	Intrinsic quality	⚡ Perceived quality
Engineering and design	Long lead times	⚡ Responsiveness and short lead time
	Few models, ranges	⚡ Multiple models
	Standardization	⚡ Bespoke
Purchasing	Standardization	⚡ Bespoke
	Price	⚡ Quality
	Routine	⚡ Flexibility

Activity/department	Their emphasis	Marketing's emphasis
Production	Long lead times	⚡ Short lead time
	Long runs	⚡ Short runs
	Standardization	⚡ Bespoke
	Ease of manufacture	⚡ Customer appeal
	Average quality	⚡ High quality
Finance and accounting	Hard and fast budgets	⚡ Flexibility
	Cost plus pricing	⚡ Market pricing
	Standardized deals	⚡ Discounts and 'specials'
Distribution and delivery	Fixed schedules	⚡ Adaptable schedules
	Low stocks	⚡ High stocks
	Limited number of warehouses	⚡ High levels of availability

Flash points ⚡

To sum up

It is important to build into the firm's operations a marketing organization that works consistently and effectively over time. Introducing this is not a one-off event which immediately produces spectacular triumphs or failures. It is more likely to lead to a shift in the direction and emphasis of the firm's entire operations. It will steadily improve performance. The key to success lies in:

1 Top management commitment
2 Preparation and planning
3 The internal effectiveness of the marketing department or operation
4 Successful integration of marketing with other parts of the firm

These hold true whether the firm employs two or two hundred workers. Inevitably the detail will change as the firm grows or changes, but the key to success remains the same commitment to the approach and its consequences.

You will need to break down traditions. This is best done during buoyant periods. Don't expect the new marketing department to save the firm when the receiver is on his way! It must be a positive step forward not a last ditch hope.

In building marketing into small firm operations, success depends on adapting the structure around the commercial strengths of the smaller firm and its market. Try to avoid the rigidity and bureaucratic attitudes which can be linked with this type of development. The most effective marketing is **customer orientated, flexible, creative, open and competitive** – one might say the same about the most effective of smaller firms.

Action Guidelines _____

1 Using a simple chart-type arrangement, describe the firm's current marketing and sales organization.

2 On the same basis, describe as fully as possible the structure adopted by a leading competitor.

3 Indicate the competitive advantages of each approach. Do this in terms of the market-place, not internal administration.

Self   *Rival(s)*

_____   _____

_____   _____

_____   _____

_____   _____

_____   _____

4 When was the last attempt in the firm to examine comprehensively the firm's marketing organization?

0 – 1 year ago   ☐

2 – 5 years ago   ☐   ☑ as appropriate

6 – 10 years ago   ☐

never   ☐

5 Identify the *industry success factors* relevant to your firm or its markets. (These may vary if the firm is operating in a number of different markets.)

Add in additional
factors if necessary

(1) _____

(2) _____

(3) _____

6 Indicate the ways in which each factor is reflected organizationally.

Factor   *Organization*

_____   _____

_____   _____

_____   _____

_____   _____

_____   _____

7 Detail a recent occasion on which the current structure capitalized on either a particular external need or industry success factor to win a meaningful piece of business.

_____

_____

_____

_____

8 Is the current organizational structure based on:

Function? ☐

Product? ☐

Market? ☐

☑ as necessary

9 Indicate the reasons for this as related to your firm today.

_____

_____

_____

_____

47

10 If *you* are the marketing organization, specify:

   (a) Proportion of time spent predominantly on marketing.

   <u>   %   </u>

   (b) Framework you use for structuring approach to the market.
   (Functional, product or market)

   _____

   _____

   _____

   _____

11 If *you* are the marketing organization:

   (a) Detail the back-up you receive.

   _____

   _____

   _____

   _____

   (b) Indicate whether this back-up is sufficient to provide the inputs needed for marketing effectiveness.

   _____

   _____

   _____

   _____

12 In introducing a marketing organization into the firm, have you:

   (a) Thoroughly researched the needs? `Yes/No`

   (b) Briefed all those likely to be affected? `Yes/No`

   (c) Conducted a training and development programme to enhance awareness and understanding of marketing? `Yes/No`

   (d) Defined a clear position for marketing with lines of access, authorities and responsibilities clearly defined? `Yes/No`

   (e) Identified the organizational flash points? `Yes/No`

   (f) Developed mechanisms for resolving any conflicts created by flash points? `Yes/No`

5
Planning: How to do it

- 'Plans are nothing: planning is everything.'
  (Dwight D. Eisenhower)
- **The marketing plan draws together the resources of the firm and matches them against marketing opportunities to provide a clear sense of purpose and direction.**
- **Marketing planning gives a solid core around which the full potential of the firm can be realized without stifling creativity and flexibility.**

Introduction and aims

Few aspects of marketing are approached with greater reluctance by managers of smaller firms than marketing planning. In a sense this is perfectly understandable, as their strengths often lie in their *flexibility, speed of response* and *ability to adapt* to changing circumstances and customer needs. If marketing planning interferes with these, it would be a very dubious asset.

The worries about marketing planning are reinforced by the jargon and mystique with which some planners surround their work. The vast indigestible tomes produced in some corporations create an inevitable feeling of scepticism in any owner or manager of a small firm. However, the difference between the outward appearance of certain plans and the underlying reality behind planning should never be confused. Properly drawn up, plans need not be turgid or difficult to understand. Correctly employed, there is no need for planning to reduce the effectiveness of the core talents of a smaller firm.

The intention of this unit is to bring out the reality which underpins all effective planning. Here the emphasis is on *planning*. The plan

49

itself is primarily a written statement reflecting hard work and providing a clear means of reference. This is not to underplay the importance of a document entitled 'The Marketing Plan'. Most firms embarking on this process gain enormously from the discipline of the drafting process and the control systems which should emerge from it.

Effectiveness involves three interrelated elements:

1 Understanding
2 Development
3 Execution

How are these features moulded into a finalized plan?

Myths and realities

A serious attempt to introduce marketing planning into any smaller firm should start by stripping it of the elaborate mythology which has been built up. Planning is drawing up:

> A set of actionable guidelines for the firm's future development based on a proper understanding of its true marketing potential.

Shorn of jargon, drawn up in a constructive and creative way, plans provide the solid basis on which all the firm's assets can be effectively exploited.

Apply a few simple rules of thumb:

- **Plans are working documents** – anything which interferes with this is redundant.
- A short and simple plan will be more valuable than a long complex plan.
- Documents produced individually without involving others are testaments not plans.

Meeting these criteria should lead to plans which can be adapted to circumstances, redrawn if necessary, and learnt from.

The workaday role of plans makes a number of demands on those producing them. First, avoid the elaborate documents often produced by large firms at the start of a new financial/trading year.

These are seldom used from the time they are agreed or approved by the board. They gather dust until the next occasion when plans are required.

The marketing plan should be one of the most heavily used and frequently consulted documents produced within the firm.

The managing director of a Leeds based footwear company produced a four-page plan which was stuck to the top of his desk for constant reference and use.

A firm of engineering consultants had their plan reproduced so that it could be kept in the wallet of every key executive.

The plan should be in a form which allows any manager seeking to make a marketing decision to refer to it and benefit from it.

This means that the second rule of thumb gains added significance. Long and complex plans cannot be used in the way described above. It is essential that the written plan is kept down to only a few pages. This is not a way of cutting down the work involved in planning – the opposite is usually true. Time still needs to be invested in developing ideas, exploring them and working out their potential pay-offs. However, the final outcome should be refined to the shortest and most precise form.

An individual, no matter how talented, left to his own devices to produce 'The Plan', will seldom be able to refine it enough. A team effort is required. Even if there is only one marketing decision maker in the firm, he should seek to try out his ideas, test his beliefs and seek advice and insight from others during the planning process. True, the final worked out plan will be his effort, but planning is a group activity. The final, refined plan should be tested on others and a determined effort made to probe for alternatives, contingencies and the risks if assumptions do not work out in practice.

Building the plan

So far a great deal of emphasis has been laid on the importance of adopting a systematic approach to marketing. This is particularly true of marketing planning. Planning is iterative, involving returning to earlier issues and decisions if new factors emerge or need to be assimilated.

The elements in a plan need be no more complex or involved than the following headings:

The audit of resources and potential

The objectives, simple, concise but recognizing alternatives

The target market(s), specified in as much detail as the search for operational conclusions allows

The marketing strategy

The tactics, identified within the overall strategy to translate ideas into action

The framework of budgets, costs, timings and controls

The framework for evaluation

The research into the market required to fill gaps, give clues and develop knowledge

This is a suggested framework, not a strait-jacket

It is best to work within a 'rolling' plan – revising it at perhaps quarterly intervals, but keeping the period at, say, a year. The precise timetable and scale should be designed around the company and the market conditions it faces. However, as a broad guideline, it is probably not sensible to plan for less than a year, while more than three years ahead will be highly speculative – with the possible exception of capital goods, agricultural and mining industries.

The marketing audit

A very useful way to start is with the Marketing Audit, sometimes called 'the appreciation' which is similar in fuction to the financial audit carried out as normal practice by virtually all firms. In time the marketing audit will be just as much a part of the annual company routine. It is a systematic review of resources, strengths (assets) and weaknesses (liabilities).

A marketing audit will only be effective if carried out from the perspective of the market, with the firm's ability to meet customer needs central. The two elements of this are:

1 A picture of the company's overall market(s), plus any broad environmental forces likely to affect it.

2 A summary statement of the firm's competitive position. SWOT analysis (Strengths, Weaknesses, Opportunities and Threats) can be very helpful here.

It is useful to draw up a picture of the firm's markets along the lines of Figure 9.

Figure 9 *The interaction between the different environments and the marketing system.*

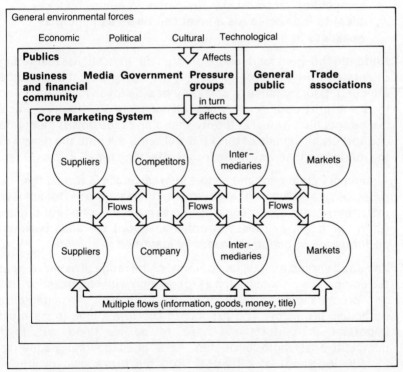

Flows: information, goods, money, title, services

This will bring out:

(a) General environmental forces such as changes in technology which can affect the firm, its supplies or customers. The inability of firms such as Gestetner producing spirit duplicators to react to new systems of photocopying and word processing illustrates the importance of this.

(b) The role of different wider 'publics' to influence a firm's future: a bad publicity from the media has crippled many firms. Failure to predict or react soon enough to cuts in government spending affected numerous suppliers.

(c) The Core Marketing System which provides a future of immediate relationships. It is surprising how seldom small firms *systematically* examine their competitors or the competition faced by key customers. A failure by a key client to hold on to his market can be as damaging as a weakness in the supplier itself.

Although this general description is useful in itself, the marketing orientated firm will seek to identify with precision the elements affecting it, for instance, a company heavily involved in supplying local authority goods or services will not generalize about 'politics' but be specific on local authority spending or the government rate support grant. Details of this kind will bring out both the nature of the market and the way these forces affect the firm.

A summary statement and simple internal analysis should then be produced including an assessment of past efforts to achieve marketing goals. This means making some assumptions about the future, with the key lessons obtained about the links between *performance* → *action* → *response* identified.

The audit should include an appraisal of the range of experience at the company's disposal, such as for dealing with certain industries or customers, even markets (especially overseas), and in handling particular problems. The aspects of the firm's operations most important to performance need to be identified and their competitive strength evaluated. This goes beyond people to include judgment of offerings, both the firm's own products, services or processes and those of their main customers.

In industrial, commercial and some consumer markets the struggle for long-term profitability calls for suppliers to be in a position to audit major customers (or potential clients) almost as fully as themselves. This audit contains two particular features:

1 *Customer Audit*
2 *Relationship Diagnosis*

The customer audit should be extensive enough to include:

client's business profile	mix of customers
pattern of business	repeat buying pattern
market share	competitive picture

Often, discernible trends or patterns can provide a better picture of a company's performance than data for a fixed point in time.

The relationship diagnosis is particularly significant in service industries or in sectors in which the service role is critical to business. Here, most accounts that move do so because existing suppliers lose them through over-confidence, neglect or simply failure to spot warning signs put out by customers.

Much of the effort invested in the internal audit will be based on certain assumptions about the character and nature of the firm's business. These *key business beliefs* should be clearly stated and assessed:

A car dealer in the North East of England held as the 'key business belief' that their market for new cars (given suburban location, etc) was dominated by local, long-established private customers. To meet the perceived needs of this group, the firm invested heavily in quality checks and high service levels but at high prices. This 'quality' car emphasis was viewed as critical to maintain the high rates of repeat purchase.

A steady decline in volume sales plus a reduced average order value forced the owner to examine the market critically. He found major changes in the market-place and his business. The most dramatic was a drop in repeat sales from 60% to 20% of new car sales. A host of factors accounted for this – change in the area's population structure, declining competitiveness of his franchise and rapid growth in the proportion of his traditional market getting company cars. Repeat business now consisted largely of second-hand small cars for wives.

You will need to do an analysis of the firm's Strengths, Weaknesses, Opportunities and Threats (SWOT), divided into three parts.

1 *Current Position* Current Trading Patterns and Performance incorporating sales volume, value by product, process or service offering and customer or customer industry. Include trend data wherever possible and market shares. **Improving market shares is normally the best route to profits for smaller firms** (the exception being when the firm has a massive share in a small market).

2 *Competitive Position* This should lead from the market share analysis. The key existing and sought after customers should be identified and current buying patterns analysed. At the same time, major competition (not only the most local or obvious) should be noted and, if possible, a SWOT conducted on them.

Trends and patterns are vital here. Major developments should be included. An industrial customer may be starting in-house production or a loyal buyer for a local authority retiring – what are the implications?

3 *The Market* This can involve analysis of the firm's total market, the various segments (different regions, areas, customer groups and related needs) and the features likely to influence the business the company can win.

A small firm has the advantage of being able to include all those directly involved in its marketing in this analysis. Often this will eliminate the easy answers such as 'cut price to win this account'. The true complexity but real scope for winning *good* business should emerge.

It is often useful take a sideways look at your competitive position. This means asking how it looks to someone producing the same or similar products elsewhere but capable of moving into *your* market.

The primary purpose of the audit is to free management to think about 'Where are we now?', 'Why are we here?', 'How are we doing?' and 'Where are we going?'.

This last ought to be inseparable from the challenge 'Where do we want to go?' or, more specifically, 'What are the company's objectives?'

Objectives

The forces described in the audit will be driving the firm in certain directions. Sales forecasts, judgements, perhaps some market research will play a part in defining the broad direction in which the firm is moving. This appraisal needs to be matched against the objectives of the company.

Objectives are management's judgements about where *it* wants the firm to be. Ambition requires that there is a gap between the position the firm will be in 'naturally' and the results of determined marketing action. There is generally an implicit aim – to use objectives to 'stretch' the firm and its staff to their full potential.

Arriving at the specific objectives, for a small firm, is normally a personal process, particularly where the owner's entrepreneurial insight is a key factor to corporate success. The owner manager of a kitchen furniture company in North Lancashire illustrated this with the emphatic comment that in *his* firm the direction taken would be decided by him.

Having said this, the characteristics that marketing objectives should have can be identified.

Objectives ought to be:
- **Clear**   State objectives simply, briefly and with a minimum of ambiguity.
- **Communicable**   Successful execution will usually be in the hands of others. Their ability to be effective will largely depend on how well they understand their objectives.
- **Actionable**   This is probably the single most important feature. The firm ought to be clear that with existing

resources and skills, the objectives set are realistic.

- **Internally consistent**   It is very easy to set objectives which, although individually acceptable, run counter to each other. Unnecessary clashes or conflicts undermine the entire process.
- **Quantifiable**   Wherever possible the clarity and precision of numbers should be built into objectives, partly to give a greater sense of direction and partly to give a basis for proper evaluation of performance.

These should be firmly based within a marketing framework and focused on the key areas of offering, customer and market.

Warning note   Setting too many objectives can be fatal, as many will contain stated or implicit sub-objectives. In the light of this, most firms are wise to set only three or four overall marketing objectives. Achieving these will depend on the combination of strategies and tactics adopted.

Strategy

The firm's strategy outlines broadly how management sees the firm achieving its overall objectives and goals. It emerges from an appraisal of the best way of taking the company forward to achieving these in a coherent way. Clarity and succinctness pay off here.

In drawing up the strategy the firm should not grasp at the one approach but clearly *identify* and *review* alternatives.

These should then be assessed in terms of their:
- Interaction with goals
- Risk
- Cost
- Probability of effectiveness
- Demands on resources

Once embarked upon, a particular strategy will establish the position of the firm in the market. It should lead clearly into specific tactics for execution

Target market(s)

Successful marketing is generally marked by skilful matching of the firm's product or services against a particularly appropriate or relevant market. Identification of the key customer group around which the product or service, in the widest definition, will be built, is critical.

The target market(s) should be fully spelt out in terms of:
- Location
- Trading characteristics
- Back-up and service level requirements
- Technical or performance needs
- Image and presentation demands
- Purchasing behaviour, notably price and credit criteria

This combination should be reviewed in the light of company strategy and objectives. Occasionally the processes of identifying the target market and its needs will call for additional information or *market research.* This should be noted in the plan.

Tactics

The tactics identify the specific policies and actions to be undertaken by the firm within the strategy to achieve its objectives. As indicated earlier, these will focus on customers, markets and offerings.

The target market(s) should be specified and the nature of their needs identified.

A South East based technical and research laboratory identified three basic customer groups for their export services:

59

- UK firms seeking information and approval for foreign technical standards.
- Foreign firms seeking approvals for British Standards.
- Other research laboratories and firms seeking specialized equipment.

Assuming that tackling all three fell within the strategy of the firm, different tactics would be needed to open up these markets.

Tactics, in this sense, centre on the policies adopted in the marketing mix areas of: offering (product, service and process), promotion, price and distribution. The design of the mix is discussed in Unit 13. The specific actions to be conducted in each area should be explored.

The firm just mentioned might increase the range of their service by establishing a reciprocal arrangement with a continental laboratory to pass on specialized overseas testing. Promotion could be arranged through a joint exhibition or symposium, charging a low handling fee to stimulate business and seeking to process enquiries very quickly to establish high levels of repeat buying.

The combination of these tactics and ther interrelationships is central to their effectiveness. In order to ensure successful implementation, an *action programme* can be drawn up highlighting the interplay and the scheduling of activities. An action plan is most useful when it provides a general framework for action.

Budgets and controls

The earlier discussions provide guidelines which will enable the manager to identify likely expenditures, projected reviews and control procedures to be adopted in the face of any problems. One of the recurrent problems of marketing is the tendency to see it as a cost but not a revenue centre.

A Northern glass products firm overcame this by making both production and marketing profit centres with costs and revenues.

Throughout the budgeting process you ought to bear clearly in mind that expenditure levels are set to achieve certain ends. The necessary funds should be put aside. When you cannot afford to spend this money, alternative tactics or strategies should be drawn up or goals revised. Failure to match aims against your resources can derive as much from over-ambitious goals as from inadequate resources. Within this framework you must monitor progress and recognize and act on failure.

Planning: an iterative process

In drawing up the detail of a plan, many of the manager's original assumptions, ideas and decisions will be brought into question. Those involved in the process should be willing to go back and examine their past experiences and review them. They may need to recast their original propositions or re-examine subsequent policies (see Figure 10).

Figure 10   *Marketing planning process*

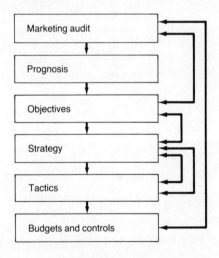

To sum up

Planning is fundamental to effective marketing. It forces managers to think long and hard about their firm and its current and likely position in the market. A format is provided here which seeks to enable the top manager of the smaller firm to capitalize on the positive attributes of planning while not undermining the strengths of his own firm.

Two riders should be introduced here:

- The best plans are often brief, characterized more by hard thinking than laboured writing.
- The creative dimension, so important to the entrepreneur's success, should not be ignored.

Action Guidelines _____

1 Briefly indicate the current 'key business belief'.

_____

_____

_____

_____

2 By volume or (taking inflation into account) by value, detail:

                         2 yrs. earlier   last yr.   this yr.   next yr.

(a) The firm's overall sales
(b) The industry's overall
    sales
(c) The nearest competi-
    tor's overall sales

Using the same criteria (volume or value) for major offerings (products/services) and customer industries, indicate the percentage change over the last year.

Customer / Offering	(i)	(ii)	(iii)	(iv)	(v)	Total
(i)						
(ii)						
(iii)						
(iv)						
(v)						
Total						

3 Detail the firm's major marketing

Strengths   (i)
               (ii)
               (iii)
               (iv)
Weaknesses   (i)
               (ii)
               (iii)
               (iv)

Opportunities (i)
                 (ii)
                 (iii)
                 (iv)
Threats   (i)
                 (ii)
                 (iii)
                 (iv)

4 For three major competitors, indicate their:

		(A)	(B)	(C)
Strengths	(i)			
	(ii)			
	(iii)			
Weaknesses	(i)			
	(ii)			
	(iii)			
Opportunities	(i)			
	(ii)			
	(iii)			

5 On the basis of *serious consideration* of two profitable current accounts, two previously profitable (but now held by a competitor listed above) and two 'desired' (but never held) accounts, indicate the *supplier* strengths and weaknesses most important to them.*

	Strengths	Weaknesses
Current (A)		
Current (B)		
Lost (A)		

Lost (B) _____   _____

_____   _____

Sought (A) _____   _____

_____   _____

Sought (B) _____   _____

_____   _____

_____   _____

6 On the basis of this analysis and others, briefly summarize 'the keys to business development' in your trade.

_____

_____

_____

_____

_____

_____

_____

_____

7 On the basis of this, indicate the practical steps that can be taken to make the firm more competitive in the eyes of the customers above.

_____

_____

_____

_____

_____

_____

_____

_____

8 Briefly state the firm's marketing objectives over the next year.

Objective   Are they?

Clear Communicable Actionable Internally consistent Quantified

(a) _____ ☐ ☐ ☐ ☐ ☐

    _____

(b) _____ ☐ ☐ ☐ ☐ ☐

    _____

(c) _____ ☐ ☐ ☐ ☐ ☐

    _____

(d) _____ ☐ ☐ ☐ ☐ ☐

    _____

9 State the overall marketing strategy to be adopted in achieving these goals.

_____

_____

_____

_____

_____

_____

_____

10 Indicate the alternatives and the reasons for their rejections.

_____

_____

_____

_____

_____

_____

11 Describe the target market(s) against which the marketing effort will be directed. As much detail as is possible and useful should be given with names, buying patterns, service required, prices paid and promotional back-up included.

	Name	Pattern	Service	Price	Other
(1)	___	___	___	___	___
	___	___	___	___	___
(2)	___	___	___	___	___
	___	___	___	___	___
(3)	___	___	___	___	___
	___	___	___	___	___

12 Specify the ways this data is gathered and how it might be improved.

_____

_____

_____

_____

_____

13 List with timing and budgets the tactics to be adopted to achieve the above objectives within the strategy described.

_____

_____

_____

_____

_____

14 Clearly show how these constitute a concerted plan and campaign to improve marketing performance with the firm's resources.

_____

_____

_____

_____

_____

6

Acting on Plans

- The real pay-offs from plans lie in their execution not production.
- Implementing plans is neither easy nor automatic.
- Learning the lessons of putting plans into action is essential if future plans are to be improved.

Introduction and aims

Part of the frustration shown by many managers in planning is caused by the gap which often seems to exist between the 'theoretical' exercise of designing, developing and drafting plans and the hard knocks of everyday trade. In part, this derives from the persistent view that plans are paper exercises never referred to or returned to, once completed. Equally, the plans produced often play down the realities of implementation, degenerating into a form of 'ideal world' aspiration. Success lies in drafting plans that can be executed and building into the plan clear mechanisms for implementation, control and execution.

Developing and drafting the plan

Success is based on recognition that the final written document or plan is far less important than the process of planning underpinning it. For this reason, outsiders can seldom if ever be brought in to do the job. Consultants may provide a gloss or structure, but they cannot replace internal management. In the overwhelming majority of smaller firms only the chief executive has the authority and knowledge to do this. His authority is critical.

68

Despite that, a wider, 'team' involvement is necessary at different stages. If numbers permit, a marketing planning group should be set up in the firm. This should involve at least three people, preferably including one outsider. This person should have some knowledge of the firm and its operations. The group should reflect both the firm's operations and the spheres of activity indicated in the SWOT analysis described earlier.

A very small firm in Crewe (4 employees) used the owner, one other worker, the owner's wife and a local banker.

A larger firm in Carlisle involved the owner, the production manager and the sales manager.

A Bradford based company involved the owner, his son, the designer, the marketing director and a professor from a nearby university.

The Audit of resources must be completed. The chief executive ought normally to give this task to one of the other participants. The brief should be to produce an honest 'risk free' appraisal to be examined in total confidence by the others. Open discussion within the group of this Audit is vital if objectives and strategy are to be drawn up. This discussion should be drawn together at a meeting of the marketing planning group – away from the factory or offices. The conclusions, that is the written Audit, should be drawn up after this *by the chief executive.*

At the same time, the Marketing Objectives, Strategy and Target Market(s) should be stated. These should be judged against the criteria indicated earlier. The chief executive needs to circulate these to the other team members asking them to consider such questions as:

(a) Are these consistent with the Audit?

(b) Do they meet the criteria indicated in the **Action Checklist?**

(c) Do superior alternatives **based on the audit** exist?

(d) Do they cope well with the possible trading conditions?

(e) Are they as brief and as clear as possible?

This discussion should produce the first part of the marketing plan.

Those operationally responsible for achieving the objectives against the target markets and within the strategy should then be informed of these and asked to comment on three things:

- The objectives, target markets and strategy
- The tactics which should be adopted and their personal *and* departmental role in achieving them. This should include timings and costs.
- The control and evaluation of performance.

Where specific product, service or market responsibilities exist, it may only be necessary to inform those involved in them of that part of the plan.

The chief executive should draw these elements together. Everyone responding to the above should be involved in this review and their observations and reactions to them acknowledged and discussed. The quickest way to erode commitment to this area is to ignore it.

The final plan will now be taking shape. In all likelihood it will be too long and too complex. It should be viciously edited with only key issues which NEED to be included kept. This version should be distributed to all those involved in its execution, accompanied by a *clear* note of their contribution. Unless those involved are clear about the expectations held of them, they will seldom work to their full potential.

Implementation

Ensuring that those involved in implementing the plan accept and understand their roles is only the first step in implementation. Built into the plan should be *key performance criteria* which should be identified, then routinely monitored and assessed. Significant or unexpected deviations can be noted and examined.

Normally a 'rolling plan' should be adopted. This means that, although regular updates and reviews are critical, the plan is rolled forward so that the practical time horizon remains at a year. This does not mean that rigorous, critical appraisals of performance cannot take place, merely that they are built into and do not disrupt performance.

Effective implementation means identification of clear responsibilities, tasks and targets linked to time scales, those responsible being named, even including the chief executive. The greater the direct involvement in setting tasks, the greater the likelihood of their achievement.

Market shares

Effectiveness will depend on the firm's ability to convert planned policies into competitive success. An essential element in this competition is the struggle for *market share.* There is mounting evidence that *profitability increases with market share.*

In one report it was estimated that return on investment for businesses with less than 10 per cent of a market was approximately 9 per cent. In contrast, firms with shares exceeding 40 per cent had a return on investment of 30 per cent – over three times that of smaller share firms.

This poses special problems for those smaller firms who do not know their market share, which may come from a failure to define their market carefully – something that should be done at an early stage. Once understood, the challenge of increasing the company's share can be built into operations with direct implications for profits. This profit appraisal and analysis is an integral element in effective implementation of marketing plans.

Action Guidelines ──────────

1 Identify those responsible for developing and drafting plans.

_____

_____

_____

_____

_____

2 Highlight the special attributes, in terms of SWOT analysis knowledge of the market or other features, that each brings to the planning.

_____

_____

_____

_____

_____

3 State the dates for initial meetings and reviews.

_____

_____

_____

_____

_____

4 Review the objectives, target market and strategy along the lines identified in Unit 5.

_____

_____

_____

_____

_____

(a) _____

_____

(b) _____

_____

(c) _____

_____

(d) _____

_____

(e) _____

_____

5 Name those operationally responsible for achieving these
   objectives. Note interrelationships and overlaps.

_____

_____

_____

_____

6 Bring out any difficulties highlighted by those named above (5).

_____

_____

_____

7 Are any revisions necessary? | Yes/No |

   If YES, which? _____

_____

_____

_____

8 Detail, unambiguously, the *key performance criteria* by sector of
   activity, product, service or market.

_____

_____

_____

_____

9 Give the dates on which review sessions will take place.

   (1) _____

   (2) _____

   (3) _____

   (4) _____

Section 2

The Benefits of Gathering and Using Information

7

Information for Business Development

- Information is as valuable as capital, machinery or land.
- Making information work harder for the firm will improve returns at very low costs.
- Only through mobilizing the firm's resources of information and knowledge, can the company successfully plan and make effective decisions.

Introduction and aims

Many successful managers have a divided view of marketing information or intelligence. On the one hand, there is personal, highly specific information (usually culled from 'the grapevine' or simply 'contacts'). On the other hand, there is the more formal, probably less specific data usually identified with non-personal sources or in reports or books, usually summarized as marketing research.

Assessment by these same managers frequently follows predictable lines. The personal, 'grapevine' material is highly rated. Some, particularly with a sales background, will attribute much of their success to the access to, and use of, this material. At the same time, the formal data is generally viewed with suspicion and either rejected because it is 'too general', 'too widely available' or disbelieved because it is at variance with accepted knowledge.

In making this division, managers are doing themselves and their firms a disservice. The different forms of data available can all play a useful part in building business. Personal data may be immediate, specific and lead to clear lines of action but is seldom open to cross-checking and is likely to be biased and difficult to use to build into an overall picture of the market. The non-personal data has virtually the opposite strengths.

A company which is serious about understanding its market, needs to organize its handling of both types.

Organizing information

Simply collecting data is a pretty pointless activity. Despite that, it is common to find small firms with enormous mountains of useless and unused data tying up space, costing money in storage and, because of the volume, preventing any effective use being made of the residue of valuable material. For these reasons, the most valuable first stage in organizing information is frequently a massive *data reduction* exercise.

There are three steps in data reduction
- Build a picture of the material that exists.
- Identify ways of reducing it to manageable and usable proportions.
- Store or destroy the rest.

An *information inventory* should be conducted at approximately annual intervals. This should indicate the material which is available, the reasons why retained and, if possible, the executive responsible for its use. The critical data probably refers to:

- The firm itself
- The competition
- Suppliers (own and competitors)
- Intermediaries (actual and possible)
- End customers
- Influencers of the market (media, government, pressure groups, trade associations, etc.)
- Wider determinants of trade (economic, technological, cultural and political forces)

In organizing the material, it is useful to divide it into 'Nice to know' and 'Need to know'. The latter should be clearly identified and regularly evaluated.

The first inventory conducted by the firm should be carefully collated. In very small firms a *marketing 'fact book'* will suffice. The value of this will depend largely on the extent to which it is of a size and in a form which lends itself to easy use. In other small firms the volume of operational data may demand more substantial methods of storage. Here, a specific member of the firm should be given responsibility for managing this data.

A number of simple disciplines can be employed in reducing this to manageable proportions. There is a strong tendency to include a considerable amount of surplus data. This can lie in the temptation to take numbers themselves to levels of 'accuracy' which add little to understanding. (See Figure 11.)

Figure 11   *Data reduction: a simple first step*

Percentage of total sales to particular customers		
Customer	Detailed	Simplified
A	3.09	3
B	2.41	2
C	6.74	7
D	3.39	3
E	7.22	7
F	.97	1
G	1.13	1
H	3.12	3

In this example the amount of error means that taking figures to a second decimal point is meaningless. Very little is lost in knowledge, but a great deal is gained in clarity with the simplified figures. Employing simple statistical forms of aggregation, for example means and standard deviations, can further reduce the data but add a great deal to comprehension.

Gathering information for plans and decisions

The value of information lies in the use to which it is put. It is a vital support for creative management.

This calls for a programme to ensure that information is:
- with the right person
- in the right place
- at the right time
- in a form which can be used

The corner-stone of the entire process is a well designed **marketing information system**. This should be designed to ensure an effective match of information and need.

Managers seeking to obtain and use information effectively are well advised to develop some form of systematic approach to *decision making* and *briefing*. Both these concepts require some explanation.

Developing a *systematic approach to marketing decision making* involves:

(a) Thinking through the steps that are or ought to be followed in making a decision.

This to include:

Identifying the problem
↓
Specifying the problem
↓
Reviewing alternatives
↓
Indicating major courses of action
↓
Highlighting decision criteria
↓
Specifying information needs relevant to decision criteria

(b) Refining this approach so that, although the system remains, it is uncluttered and virtually automatic.

Briefing is a neglected skill. Anyone who regularly bemoans the irrelevance or the lack of value in material which has been collected should remember that he or she provided the overall direction for its gathering.

The analogy with scientific research is worth bearing in mind. Most scientists or engineers spend at least as much time designing their research, carefully setting up the experiment, before embarking upon the test. The same care should be taken in setting up a market intelligence gathering exercise. The data processing concept 'Garbage in' (the brief) 'Garbage out' (the results) should be embedded into the process of briefing.

One practical approach to briefing is to make the brief a mirror image of the final information needed. Data already available should be included and real gaps acknowledged.

The marketing information system

Any company seeking to obtain maximum benefit from its accumulated and new information has a responsibility to ensure that it is organized and distributed in the most effective way. The information inventory is a start. It should bring out precisely the array of material available, including the 'private' stocks held by key individuals.

'Working' information has to be in the hands of those wanting to work with it. This involves a careful appraisal of the marketing organization within the firm now, in terms of the kinds of decisions made, areas of responsibility and the data **needed** to be effective in these areas. The chief executive should take both a directive and a responsive approach to this.

Being **directive** means suggesting the information needed by the individual involved. **Responsiveness** involves giving him or her the chance to indicate data required. To be effective the criteria for allocation must be 'needed to be known'.

A picture of this interacting group of persons, their information needs, and the procedures for getting it to them should be drawn up. It should be kept as simple as possible.

Once established, an orderly flow of relevant information should be organized. Hiccups, lags and delays should be avoided, as these erode the system. Otherwise it will degenerate to an expensive, valueless mess. The pattern of communication involved can be studied regularly with summary forms produced to reduce the detail held centrally or fed to top management.

At the base of the system, an expanding network of sources, rated according to value and quality should be sought. Broadly speaking, a wide base and tightly organized decision group held together by an efficient information system can generate major benefits.

Figure 12 *The marketing information system*

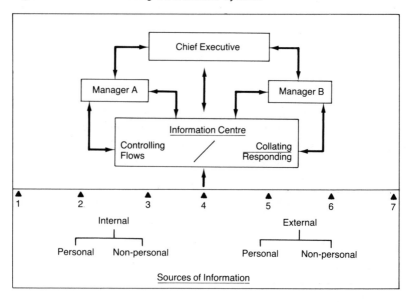

This diagram gives an overview of a method for organizing the system. Sources of information are clearly identifed (1–7). Instead of data coming into the firm in an ill-organized flow to various parts of the firm, as far as possible a single 'information centre' receives the material. This is distributed to those needing it. At the same time their responses are returned, assessed and redistributed in short and manageable forms.

Although this type of model may seem over-complex for many small firms, the basic approach of developing flows and practical procedures geared to efficiency is applicable to any firm. At present, valuable marketing data is lost or poorly appreciated only because it is poorly managed. The processes involved in gathering and co-ordinating the related information gathering process is Market Research.

To sum up

Gathering and using information in its various guises is the stock in trade of successful marketing.

It incorporates:
- casually gathered insights gleaned through wide networks of relationships
- unsolicited but highly relevant contacts and leads
- informal, relatively unstructured attempts to solve problems or overcome difficulties by looking outside or within the firm for guidance and insight
- a more formal, deliberate and structured approach to finding the answers to identified issues.

Unless information is organized, processed and a marketing intelligence system established even in a rudimentary form, an invaluable asset will be wasted. Its use is vital.

Action Guidelines _____

1 Identify the major (existent within the firm) sources of data on:

  (i) the firm's current trading pattern _____

_____

_____

    previous trade _____

_____

_____

    significant changes _____

_____

_____

    market performance (in own terms) _____

_____

_____

    market performance (in customers' eyes) _____

_____

_____

  (ii) the competition _____

_____

_____

_____

  (iii) suppliers _____

_____

_____

_____

  (iv) intermediaries _____

_____

_____

  (v) end customers _____

_____

_____

(vi) influences on the market _____

_____

_____

_____

(vii) determinants of trade _____

_____

_____

_____

2 How much of this data is currently held?

_____

_____

_____

_____

3 How far back does it go?

_____

_____

_____

_____

4 For each source, indicate when and for what it was last used.

_____

_____

_____

_____

5 Identify the marketing information which **you need to know**
   (a) regularly _____

_____

_____

_____

   (b) intermittently _____

_____

_____

_____

6 For other relevant executives, identify the information **they need to know**.

(a) _____   _____
    _____   _____
    _____   _____
                                      _____
                                      _____
                                      _____

(b) _____   _____
    _____   _____
    _____   _____
                                      _____
                                      _____
                                      _____

7 Construct a model of the steps involved in a *recent* key marketing decision.

8
How Important is Market Research?

- **Research is the corner-stone of attempts to understand and manage the firm's future.**
- **Market research builds objectivity and system into data collection.**
- **The firm has available to it a wide array of sources of information and approaches to its collection.**

Introduction and aims

During the last few years the sources, types and methods of gathering data have multiplied. When looking for relevant information on your markets you are faced with two equally daunting tasks:

1 Understanding and managing the vast amounts of data available to you.
2 Designing and implementing programmes of information gathering which *materially* improves on existing data, providing greater relevance, immediacy, confidentiality or simply improved quality.

Efficiency depends on the purpose behind the collection and the research process itself. Although a variety of sources will be identified below, their value to a specific firm will vary enormously between companies and over time.

In the majority of cases of significant marketing decisions, the right course of action is not clear and data is available or can be obtained to help provide some clues to the best solution.

This unit seeks to:

(a) indicate the various sources of information and related assistance

(b) suggest practical and, where possible, low cost ways of conducting market research.

Although the particular problems of exports and international and export trade will be dealt with later, sources of information and the special requirements of this area will be discussed here. A worked example of a market research plan using export data is provided at the end of this chapter to crystallize these issues.

Sources of information

A practical way of reviewing the places where information can be found is in terms of a matrix, relating type of material to location (See Figure 13.)

Figure 13   *Sources of information*

| | | Location | |
		Internal	*External*
Type of information	Secondary	1	3
	Primary	2	4

Faced with a marketing problem and related information, managers are advised to check out each of these in the suggested sequence – 1, 2, 3, 4. This will ensure that the more difficult and costly sources will only be tackled after easier, cheaper avenues have been tried.

Internal secondary information   This category corresponds to the data highlighted in the information inventory. It has been collected by the firm for purposes other than the current problem. It includes such routine items as: orders, enquiries, deliveries, stocks, damage rates, returns, tender documents (applications and failures), quality control and performance standards, customer lists (current and past).

It should incorporate any special analysis performed.

A toy manufacturer regularly monitored the different pattern of orders for his various lines. These were related to seasonal and regional ordering patterns. He found patterns of fashion and attitude which steadily improved his performance.

A contract engineer reviewed the relationship between enquiries and successful conversion. He found that in overseas projects it was not enough to work solely with the main contractor. He had to work with the originator of the order. However this did not mean the contractor could be ignored. Both had to be cultivated.

A small retailer found that a major determinant of sales for brands was physical proximity to the 'brand leaders' in particular areas. Placing a slow mover next to the best seller boosted sales with no noticeable loss to the brand leader.

The basic data and previous analyses can be matched against the current enquiry. When this does not resolve this question, new studies can be conducted.

A firm with declining orders might find the damage rates or returns increasing. The problem could be deteriorating standards or new delivery systems. The earlier the problem is spotted, the less harm will be done.

A consultancy, with worsening success rates with proposals, could discover that increasing contact rates reflect lack of client selectivity. Higher costs are being incurred but to no avail. Without research, subsequent efforts can go down the wrong track completely, with enormous wastage.

A Scottish firm wasted a vast amount of effort searching out new enquiries when its problem was not enquiry rate but very low conversion from enquiry to order. It had spent £10,000 before realizing that reducing the order processing time from six weeks to three quadrupled the conversion rate – and cost nothing!

Internal primary information This involves enquiries within the firm specifically set up to answer questions about particular issues. It can involve quizzing staff or gathering new information from existing systems. Central to this are the sales staff. These have been rightly described as the eyes and ears of the company. Although their primary role as sales people should never be lost, their knowledge and access to customers, distributors and competitors ought to be tapped. Despite their significance, other sources can be equally important – technical, design and account staff might be able to obtain data unavailable in other ways.

A West Country based fastener company asked its delivery staff to 'spot' and report on the deliveries of rivals.

A London based engineering consultancy regularly asked its experts in different fields to review with clients and contacts new market developments.

A Nottingham retailer used its display and merchandising staff to tour other shops and report on new trends.

For exporters, the British Overseas Trade Board can provide special support for firms with internal staff able to do market research professionally. Under specific circumstances a high proportion of the costs can be obtained for projects conducted outside the EEC (see proposal at end of chapter for this model).

External secondary information Generally the search for additional insight on the market-place will mean going outside the company for data. A major feature of the information revolution mentioned earlier is the proliferation of organizations dedicated to collecting, distributing, selling and in other ways making information available.

It is outside the firm (*external*) and *secondary* in that it has been collected for other purposes. Some is static and stored in conventional forms – reports, books, directories, etc. Increasing amounts are being handled by new technologies such as Prestel, Ceefax, Oracle, On-Line Data-bases (for example Lockheed).

There is a proliferation both in type and volume of data. The next few years are likely to transform this as an even more recent development – 'Interactive Systems' – emerges. This means that the enquirer will be able to ask questions, react to responses and ask for different or modified answers.

External primary information All too often even the most rigorous search of the secondary sources will expose gaps, leaving areas requiring research geared to the specific problem faced. This process of gathering external primary information is largely the preserve of market research.

Two points should be kept in mind:

- The fundamental requirements of good market research are relatively simple – discipline, objectivity and system. Its underlying ethos lies in the attempt to introduce science to marketing. The jargon surrounding it contributes little to this.

- Equally, applying relatively simple principles frequently requires considerable expertise and occasionally leads to specialization.

Well conducted market research can provide invaluable insights. Occasionally you can do this yourself if you apply discipline, objectivity and system. Often it costs less – in real terms – to get someone else to do it. Generally in such circumstances, companies are strongly recommended to use a company listed in the Market Research Society Handbook. Using and choosing an outside agency calls for the application of some stern disciplines. In general, the professionalism and overall quality of the researcher's work matches that of the person setting the task.

In organizing a market research project, the first steps are the same whether the company intends doing it itself or using an outsider. Even when a professional is used to it, it is worth understanding many of the issues in design and execution.

Earlier it was emphasized that the foundations of good market research lie in identifying and specifying the problems or questions at issue besides noting the options open and insights needed for choice. This is not a casual, ad hoc process. It should be written down, checked, modified and adapted as necessary until it is an easily understood unambiguous statement.

The material collected in the earlier stages of the research ought now to be matched against this. Some questions might be answered. Unanticipated problems or issues may emerge. Updating may be necessary. New sources of information or assistance can be identified. Most usefully, the problems, decisions and choice criteria should be increasingly refined, firmed up, simplified and clarified. Occasionally, direct insights into the way the research might be tackled will emerge.

A small educational publisher discovered that most school textbooks in his field were chosen through consultation and discussion between most teachers in a department.
Individual interviews would easily miss this 'team' feature, but group discussions were very effective at bringing out the likely response to a new series of geography books.

Having identified the issue(s) in question and taken the project as far as possible with readily available data, the problem of gathering external, primary information is faced. Always, whether doing it yourself or using someone else, prepare a thorough brief incorporating as much background as possible (without clouding the issue).

A clear statement of the objectives of the research is necessary. This should incorporate both the operational task (such as entering a new market) and the research purpose (for instance finding out how many firms are established in the market). It is normally a good idea to pass this to someone informed, but not directly involved for comment and criticism.

The task of gathering data can now be tackled. There is a fallacy that market research is solely concerned with questionnaires, interviews and related techniques. Often observation and consultation can be just as useful.

Watching how people behave in particular situations, use products or react to stimuli, can be invaluable.

A producer of stacking equipment for small warehouses

found that stores personnel claimed one method of operating in an interview but did something different in practice.

A small retail group discovered that customers claimed to follow a particular path round their shops and to do a great deal of price comparison – but observed behaviour was totally different.

A security consultant found the same gap between claim and reality. Clients claimed a vigour in selecting staff and in checking out references that bore no resemblance to reality. The same firm found a similar gap between claim and action in the use of security devices. His conclusions based on 'observed' behaviour were totally different from those which would have been prompted by recorded answers.

When an observation based study is conducted, it should be treated as a true experimental situation with:

- the issues to be tested noted
- the method of observation **stated** and **adhered** to

Ill-considered, random deviations will rapidly erode any value.

- the results clearly reported and evaluated

Observation research is not to be confused with 'keeping an eye on things'.

Consultation with outside experts can play a useful part in research, particularly into new products or services, industrial markets or highly specialized fields. In gathering technical or scientific data, specific attention should be given to identifying experts or specialists in the area. They will often be in a position to provide detailed guidance. Here again, consistency of approach and discipline differentiate this from casual discussion. Generally this means raising *the same* issues, in *the same* or a *consistent* way with more than one person. Change the question even slightly and true comparisons are not possible.

The delphi method provides a useful structure for this (see Figure 14). A small number of 'experts' (A–E) in this area are identified. The manager could include people inside the firm, from the trade association or even potential buyers. These can be asked a series of questions. The answers and comments are collected and collated ('Initial Responses'). A revised questionnaire is produced, incorporating the conclusions of the first with the results, comments and other issues raised ('Revised and Collated Responses'). The experts are consulted again, now having the new data at their disposal.

This approach has been particularly successful in speculative areas where limited experience and lack of hard data create problems.

Figure 14 *The delphi cycle*

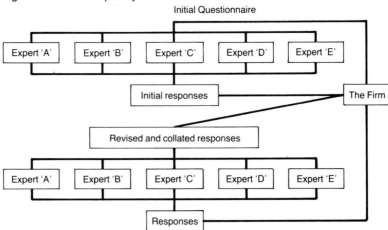

This cycle can be repeated with maximum convergence of response typically occurring on the fifth occasion.

It was used by the small team handling the arrangements for the 150th Anniversary of the Stockton–Darlington railway. They had to calculate the number of car park spaces needed for the highpoint of the celebrations – 'The Cavalcade of Steam'. Nothing like it had happened for over 25 years. With no 'hard' data to go on it was decided to use 'Delphi'. Their final estimate was only 1 per cent out, with almost 200,000 vehicles turning up eventually.

The bulk of market research involves some form of questionnaire based study of users, buyers, middlemen and those in a position to influence purchase. Discussion here will touch on the following areas of interest. The terms often associated with these are noted. The schema below assumes clear research objectives have been set:

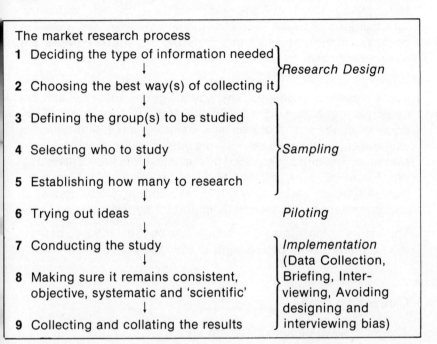

The market research process

1 Deciding the type of information needed ⎫
                ↓   ⎬ Research Design
2 Choosing the best way(s) of collecting it ⎭
                ↓
3 Defining the group(s) to be studied ⎫
                ↓   ⎪
4 Selecting who to study   ⎬ Sampling
                ↓   ⎪
5 Establishing how many to research   ⎭
                ↓
6 Trying out ideas   Piloting
                ↓
7 Conducting the study   ⎫ Implementation
                ↓   ⎪ (Data Collection,
8 Making sure it remains consistent,   ⎬ Briefing, Inter-
  objective, systematic and 'scientific' ⎪ viewing, Avoiding
                ↓   ⎪ designing and
9 Collecting and collating the results ⎭ interviewing bias)

Each of these areas involves its special skills. Before embarking on a DIY market research study, any small firm should think hard about whether the costs in time, the risks of error and the money spent is worth it. If the answer is YES, the following comments highlight some of the points to bear in mind.

What type of information do you need?

Information takes many forms. It can be hard and quantitative. This type can generally be checked or corroborated from other sources. It includes volume purchases, prices paid, delivery schedules, frequency of buying and budgets.

Sometimes data is less clearly 'hard' or easy to check. However, it can be quantitative, perhaps testable. The role or position of the respondent, his freedom of action or purchase discretion, the required features of the product or service, performance under test, plans, even current suppliers are in this category. Ambiguities, changes, even misunderstandings are possible because of the nature of this material, but the responses are generally consistent.

Research designed to gather attitudes and/or opinions poses major additional problems. The way questions are asked and the person doing it can have a direct effect on the answer given. Equally significant, attitudes and opinions are the product of experience, hence they change, become modified, even reversed over time. The difficulties faced by the researcher are increased by the reluctance, even inability, of those being quizzed to describe their attitudes, particularly those existing at lower levels of consciousness or not viewed as important by the interviewee.

The nature of the information sought has be to established early. It will be the principal determinant of the research method used.

Collecting data

The main ways of collecting data are:

1 Questioning by —— Telephone (*)
         —— Post (*)
         —— Personal Interview (*)
2 Observing by   —— Diaries
         —— Person (*)
         —— Instruments

Only those marked (*) should be seriously considered for self-designed and executed research by the small firm.

Telephone and postal approach can be very effective at gathering a great deal of 'hard' data about a restricted number of issues. Those being questioned in these ways can become very impatient of long, detailed approaches, and such methods should normally be avoided when seeking attitudes or opinions. They will, however, be surprisingly willing to give brief answers.

Personal observation can be very useful in gathering 'hard' data. Work practices, ways of using materials or machinery, reaction to in-store displays, packaging – these are typical of the issues open to study in this way.

A kitchen furniture manufacturer from East Anglia successfully redesigned the cabinets he sold based on a series of observation studies. He kept a careful diary, noting down in detail the way women used the surfaces. Having observed about thirty, he drastically changed his thinking on lay-out and design.

Attitudes and opinions are usually studied through either detailed 'in-depth' personal interviews or 'group discussions'. In conducting either of these, it is easy to lose touch with the disciplined approach required. This is particularly true when the manager (committed to, concerned about and an expert on his product or service) is studying a prospective buyer or user. The flow of discussion can easily shift a long way from the key issues being studied or, even if these remain central, the interview can start influencing responses. A firm and fixed approach is needed with:

- questions set and adhered to
- 'prompt points' included, so that if the interview moves away from the point, these are not lost.

The questionnaire   Designing the questionnaire is not a casual matter to be entered into lightly.

Designing a questionnaire

(a) *The questionnaire* should be kept short, including only things *needed*.

(b) *The questionnaires* will eventually be collated and analysed. The methods and requirements of this process should be incorporated in initial design, e.g. if it is important to know how different groups respond, the questionnaire must include the means of identification, such as name, age, sex or name, position in firm, time employed, seniority over those involved in buying.

97

However, these do take up part of the interview and cannot simply be added to an already lengthy questionnaire.

(c) *The questions* should be short, geared to a specific response and unambiguous.

Above all avoid the multiple issue question with 2, 3 or more sub-issues.

(d) *The words* used should be readily understood by the person expected to reply.

In general, the problem is not in knowing what to ask. It lies in knowing what not to ask.

All questionnaires must be 'piloted', that is, tested before full-scale study.

Who to study Precision in stating who is to be studied plays a critical part in effective research. In industrial markets it is particularly significant, as the purchasing officer or buyer may not be the main decision maker on technical specifications, quality standards, or even the timing of purchase. It may be the attitudes or opinions of top management or production staff which decide the source of supply, even when the purchasing officer places the order.

In consumer markets similar distinctions between buying and using exist. The bulk of fast moving consumer products are bought by housewives, even if consumption is by all the family members.

How many? Many small firms seeking insights into industrial, trade, local authority or government markets will be able to conduct a virtual census of the potential market. The numbers involved will be manageable. Each will represent a significant potential market. Under most normal circumstances, a census is preferable to using a small representative group as a sample.

When the numbers involved are too large for a census to be conducted, the firm will be forced to select a sample from the group in question. This will be chosen to represent the entire population. The value of the research will disappear if those chosen are untypical. The firm needs to:

1 minimize the numbers to keep costs down, while

2 making it representative.

A trial study No programme of market research should be embarked upon without a pilot or trial study. This try-out does not need to be massive or costly, but **it does need to be done.**

At the same time, it should be recognized as a test of the research methods – questionnaire, method of interview, interviewer – not a piece of exploratory research. The results, other than about methodology, should be ignored. A careful evaluation of the questionnaire, method, etc. needs to take place after the pilot, based on the issue of how well they performed the tasks required. Did those interviewed understand the questions? Was the questionnaire too long? Was the material sought available?

Conducting and controlling the study

Once finalized, the approach adopted should be rigidly adhered to. Questions should be asked in as consistent a manner as possible, avoiding the deviations and departures which seem sensible and interesting at the time, but reduce the scope for building up a consistent and coherent picture.

Internal controls are needed, even if the chief executive or top marketing man is handling or conducting the project.

Such controls are:

- A full list of those to be interviewed – produced and kept to.
- A working timetable and schedule – research should take place to a tight timetable, with deviations avoided. Organize this in advance.
- Questionnaires should be produced in numbers and ways which permit completion – *avoid* rough notes and notebooks almost as much as memory.

These disciplines may seem simple and straightforward. Unfortunately their execution calls for a very strong will.

Collecting and collating the results

Earlier it was noted that many projects call for the use of outside market research specialists. The Market Research Society of Great Britain (15 Belgrave Square, London, SW1) recommends a minimum acceptable content for a project report.

It should include:
- a clear statement of the aim of the study
- identification of the sponsor of the study and the executor
- a description of those studies (if a sample is used, the general target group needs to be identified)
- any sampling techniques used
- the timing of the work
- the methods used for gathering information
- details of those who conducted the project
- a copy of any questionnaire or its equivalent
- the results themselves – factual besides descriptive

A wise firm will normally look for:
- a wider review of the implications
- comments on problems, ambiguities or needs for further investigation

The report of a professional agency should be checked against these *minimum* criteria.

A company conducting their own project will be wise to match this. The results gathered should be written up in a professional way. A firm seeking help from the British Overseas Trade Board (see Unit 24) will be required to do this if they want a grant.

To sum up

There is such a massive volume of market information and data available to the small firm manager today that organizing and controlling it is a major management task. At the base of this system lies the data which already exists but has been gathered by others, at other times, for other purposes. Collecting this tends to be low-cost and demands relatively little time. However, it seldom exactly matches the needs of the situation. Successful market research involves taking a structured approach, eliminating questions that can be resolved easily and investing one's time very carefully in the person able to resolve issues.

In the future, the firm able to manage its knowledge of the market will be one capable of succeeding. Those unable to do this systematically will face real problems. However, it should never be ignored that many of the formal information gathering approaches used by large firms are *poor* substitutes for the rapport that the owner manager has on a daily basis with his clients.

Action Guidelines _____

1 Is the firm's internal marketing information 'fact book' up to date?

_____

_____

2 What types of market information are needed by the firm?

_____

_____

3 Identify the market and relevant technical information available for
   the appropriate industry research association(s).

_____

_____

4 List the data produced by your trade association (even if not a
   member, it can often be purchased).

_____

_____

_____

5 Indicate useful information held by the local Chamber of Commerce.

_____

_____

6 Which local university, technical college or central libraries have
   useful commercial or other material?

_____

_____

7 What is available from these libraries?

_____

_____

8 When was the last time someone from the firm discussed its
   information needs with a specialist from:
   (1) the Industry Research Association?
   (2) the Trade Association?
   (3) the Chamber?
   (4) one of these libraries?

Market Research Plan _____
(using export data)

Framework

1   **Objectives**
1.1 An exact definition of product(s) and market(s) to be researched and in what country/ies.

1.2 A clear and concise statement of the marketing problem requiring investigation.

1.3 The results in terms of marketing action.

Illustration

1.1 The purpose is to explore the market potential for extruded aluminium components for use in the construction and installation of double glazing units in domestic dwellings. The study will be confined to Holland, West Germany and France.

1.2 The increasing interest in energy conservation has led to a search for reducing heat loss in the home. In Britain a strong double glazing industry has emerged. This is divided into a number of stages – materials production, component manufacture, assembly and installation. XYZ Ltd has made significant progress in servicing this market. Considerable skill and experience have been developed. The purpose of this investigation is to explore:

1.2.1 The scope for exporting XYZ's extruded aluminium components to markets in Western Europe.

1.2.2 The market(s) on which to concentrate efforts (no more than two).

1.2.3 The overall potential in these markets in the short (next two years) and medium (next five years) terms. When possible, quantities, by volume and value will be established. However the prime purpose is to explore anticipated rate and nature of developments on a qualitative basis.

1.2.4 The structure of the market in particular – the types of contractor/installers most likely to be interested in purchasing the aluminium extrusions. It is important to establish the structure of this market – are they national concerns, e.g. Alpine (UK) or local builders and glaziers. Preliminary investigation involving considerable desk work has failed to identify large national concerns such as Alpine in either Germany or France.

1.3 In sum the problem is – do substantial markets exist or are they likely to emerge in the specific product category in a form likely to meet the marketing needs of XYZ Ltd? The results in terms of marketing action are:

1.3.1 A go/no go decision on whether to make a determined effort to penetrate these markets.

1.3.2 A clearly identified priority system for the markets on which to concentrate resources.

1.3.3 Guidance on the optimum price and promotion policies.

1.3.4 Information on the pattern of distribution to indicate the scope for penetrating the markets nationally through national contractors or regionally through local firms.

1.3.5 Indications of the optimum methods of servicing the markets to ensure long-term market growth.

Framework

2   **Information requirements**

For each product and market sector, information will be required under the following headings.

2.1   Current size of the market (value and volume).

2.2   Segmentation of the total market in terms of applications, end use sectors, geographic regions, etc.

2.3   Trends in 2.1 and 2.2 with projections as appropriate.

2.4   Competition: principal competitors, market shares, strengths and weaknesses, promotional methods, channels and costs of distribution, prices and discounts, etc.

2.5   Technical standards, import duties, quotas, other government regulations.

Illustration

2   Information requirements

2.1   The current sizes of the market(s) (trade estimates plus any official statistic). Background research to date has not identified any clearly identifiable government statistics for France in this category. Information is available on Germany and Holland, but on a piecemeal basis and is rather out of date.

2.2   Preliminary investigation has indicated strong regional patterns in France and Germany. This investigation would concentrate on identifying:

2.2.1 Major national concerns.

2.2.2 The pattern of regional installation and construction.

2.2.3 The key sectors, e.g. builders, glaziers, window frame manufacturers and specialists and their different needs and their relative importance.

2.3   The target market would need both a substantial existing market and scope for growth in the short to medium term. Preliminary research suggests that the Dutch market is the most developed today. It is important to establish the long-term prospects in all markets.

2.4   Competition (see framework – self-explanatory).

2.5   Discussions with the Department of Energy have established that no EEC standards have been set up. The specific technical requirements of the target countries would be explored. In this area growing awareness has resulted in increasing government activity, particularly through grants and assistance for installation. A full picture of these and their impact on trade will be required.

Framework

3   Research method

An outline of research method and techniques to be used in order to achieve the desired results and the degree of accuracy required for effective marketing action.

3.1   The number and type of interviews to be carried out and their distribution, i.e. by region, industry sector, size of company, etc.

3.2   Status/job/responsibility of the person to be contacted/interviewed.

3.3 Sample selection procedures.

3.4 Interview techniques to be used, e.g. structured or semi-structured, etc.

Illustration

3.1 **Research method**

3.1.1 In Holland six in-depth interviews will be carried out.
Two will be with the major national concerns already identified.
Two will be from the Amsterdam area.
Two will be from the Rotterdam area.

3.1.2 In France eleven in-depth interviews will be carried out.
Four will be national concerns or regional concerns identified as among the twenty largest contractors in France.
Two will be from the Paris region
Two will be from the Lille region.
Two will be from the Lyons region (these will be very exploratory to identify any different North/South patterns).

3.1.3 In West Germany twelve in-depth interviews will be carried out.
four will be national concerns.
Three will be in the North German Lander (Hamburg).
Three will be in the Ruhr.
Two will be in the Frankfurt region.

3.2 The interviewees will vary according to the type and size of firms. In the larger/national concerns (employing over 500 persons according to *Kompass*) the purchasing manager will be approached. In smaller firms the chief executive will be interviewed.

3.3 The sample will be selected on a 'structured–random' basis with national and regional lists identified. From the lists so identified, the sample will be selected. In all cases twice as many firms as required will be identified to allow for refusals to participate.

3.4 In all cases the interviews will be structured in the following form:
Part (a) Semi-structured, quantitative and trend information
Part (b) Unstructured in-depth investigation around a series of key themes.

Framework

5 Timing/locations

The timetable should state how many days have been allocated to the various stages of research from the initial desk research to the fieldwork, programme, listing the towns and cities to be visited in each country and the final report writing.

Illustration

5 Timing/locations

5.1 Background and desk research 5 man days (partially completed – 2 days – see comments in text). Further information from Joint Chamber of Commerce and an Institute Zimmerman research report on subject due.

5.2 Fieldwork: Holland   3 days centred on Amsterdam and Rotterdam

Germany	2 days	Hamburg
	2 days	Cologne/Bonn
	2 days	Frankfurt
	2 days	others
France	2 days	Paris
	2 days	Lille
	1 day	Lyons
	2 days	others
Total	18 days	fieldwork

Research report write up 4 days.

Total research time 27 days.

Framework

6 The researcher

Sufficient detail should be supplied as to the qualifications and experience of the personnel charged with carrying out the project to satisfy the British Overseas Trade Board's (BOTB) Export Market Research Director of their suitability for such a task. An example of previously completed research can be helpful in this (all information will be treated in confidence).

9

How to Divide the Marketing into Manageable Parts

- Understanding markets means understanding customers.
- The market is not a uniform mass.
- Targeting efforts means added value and better profits through more precise matching of customer and offering.

Introduction and aims

Marketing points the manager away from the tunnel vision involved in looking at his business purely as product or service. These are fixed entities with a finite life. It directs attention towards the needs or requirements of actual or potential buyers. These are seldom fixed. They are capable of being met in many ways. Their life span is virtually infinite. There is normally scope for development and evolution.

Such a perspective has produced another conclusion. The traditional way of defining customers, as consumers of a product or service – smokers, drivers, plastics buyers, house purchasers, computer softwear clients – was filled with problems.

In the first place it is a very poor description of those in question. It misses out vital details. It bears no resemblance to their self-image. It operates on only one aspect of the purchase decision – the product or service. Taken to its logical conclusion, this view led markets towards price based, commodity market type competition.

Target marketing seeks to reverse this, emphasizing a need to direct efforts in terms of customer diversity.

- Market Segmentation provides an overall approach and cues for the division of larger markets into more cohesive groups, with more in common and against whom more effective and diverse marketing efforts can be pitched.

This chapter explores the different ways of embarking on this process.

Market segmentation

Segmentation should never be thought of solely in terms of dividing markets up into parts with more in common than the totality. This is only half the picture. Equally important, the firm ought to be able to reach the subset with a consistent offering with special appeal to the group. This should generate greater customer satisfaction, with pay-offs in terms of prices, loyalty or simply a stronger working relationship.

Most small firms have built their business on attracting particular types of customer. They can be locals wanting high service levels or simply easy access, or customers willing to pay for special features or generally better quality. Often smallness has meant that short production runs or inconvenient jobs can be tackled. There is nothing new about the phenomenon, but building it into a practical and organized approach to the market is an innovation. Because it may already be taking place, making it a virtue, developing it and gaining new opportunities from it is frequently very profitable.

A plastics moulder of self-skinned foam had always been successful at substituting its technology for older processes. They had introduced the foam to firms using traditional materials such as wood and metals. Generally this had been a responsive, problem solving process on their part. The client usually identified a need or application and the firm found a way of giving it a tangible form. This was viewed simply as a 'natural' way of doing business.

Once the scope for turning this process into a more creative, self-directed approach to building business was recognized, new opportunities emerged. Potential customers and customer groups could be categorized and approaches designed around their particular requirements could be introduced. Three segments emerged from this 'substitution market':

(a) Traditional materials user, unaware of and hostile to plastics

(b) Traditional materials user, aware of some plastics applications but ignorant of self-skinned foam

(c) Traditional materials user, but already using and familiar with some applications of foam

The selling, service and pricing policies for each group were modified to meet their different requirements. This significantly reduced wasted effort while improving success rates.

Once the idea of dividing the market into smaller segments has been accepted, a new problem emerges. If the sole criterion is greater internal cohesion or homogeneity, there is virtually no limit to the number of sub-groups that can emerge.

To cope with and control this, four conditions for a meaningful segment have been established. It must be:

- **Measurable**
- **Reachable**
- **Substantial**
- **Open to profitable commercial development**

Any segments chosen should be checked against these criteria. A number of different approaches to segmenting markets exist.

Geographic segmentation emphasizes the location of customers. A firm might target its effort on local firms. Some companies could direct their efforts on hot countries or those with high rainfall. A Manchester firm producing water softeners emphasized hard water areas. The role of this in retailing is especially great. Some retailers are learning to use access linked to geography, so that their local advertising might be directed at all those at, say, forty minutes travelling time away.

Demographic segmentation groups customers together by age, sex, class, family size, etc. Saga Holidays brilliantly exploited the opportunity of appealing to the aged. In Scotland 'Hydros' cater for family holidays.

Industrial sectoral segmentation emphasizes the classifications in which companies are placed. A firm might target on vehicle producers, manufacturers of white goods (such as washing machines, dishwashers, refrigerators, etc.) or newer segments, like fast food caterers. Government and other statistics can give a good picture of the size, while other sources can identify the firms, even the product needs.

These approaches can be rather mechanical and artificial. Equally, they tend to lump groups together in ways appropriate to those collecting data but not those trading in the area. A number of small firms have obtained special benefits from looking at their markets in terms of *usage* and *psychology.*

Usage segmentation leads to grouping of customers in the way products and services are used. This can be in relatively simple terms such as heavy, medium and light users. More complex factors can be used which incorporate work practices, even those doing the jobs.

One Midlands engineering firm found that in private industry their products were normally handled by electricians, while in the nationalized industry plumbers had traditionally done the work in question. Their different work practices demanded very different support materials and guides on application. Recognizing this and adapting their product promotion to this generated a significant sales boost.

Psychological segmentation covers a battery of issues from the loyalty of buyers, through the search for different benefits, to the life-styles of clients. Customer loyalty is a complex phenomenon

111

but can be vital to the long-term success of a firm. In some cases it means virtual blindness to the suppliers' faults. More often it means being willing to substitute avoidance of risk for lower prices. Identifying these groups and the features in *relationships* they seek can pay massive dividends.

Market gridding

This has emerged as a practical method of dividing markets up into more manageable proportions. Often it involves bringing together two of the criteria for segmentation identified above, such as industrial category and usage.

Figure 15   *Market gridding*

Product X

Industrial category Usage	Mining	Quarry-ing	Other extractive industries	Manufac-turing	Con-struction	Transport
Heavy use/ high skill						
Light use/ high skill						
Heavy use/ low skill						
Light use/ low skill						

a foundry might use this grid to analyse the overall market, then relate this to its own performance and ability to meet the special needs of particular groups, such as heavy use/high skill construction firms. The producer can spot the group for whom his product or service is most suitable.

A manufacturer of plastic guttering and clips used a simplified form of this.

Figure 16   *The DIY plastic guttering market*

	High skill	Medium skill	Low skill 'botcher'
Very frequent use (profession)			
Frequent use (enthusiast)			
Regular use (as needed)			
Intermittent use (when forced)			

The owner identified two groups who appeared to be poorly served in the market.

1 The regular use 'botcher'
2 The very frequent use medium skill

He built up a picture of their importance in the market with rough estimates of their potential value. Having identified them as markets worth tackling, he adapted his product, the advertising and instructional material and price to their needs. With this package he set about building up a distribution network suitable for these very different markets.

Target marketing

The broad thrust of this discussion has centred on the importance of the firm directing its efforts at clearly defined and increasingly well understood customer groups. The view that 'I know my customers', 'they're my friends', 'I deal with them every day' is simply not enough any more.

In target marketing this process is taken further with a detailed picture of the links in the market. This means viewing business development as a chain of marketing linkages.

Figure 17 *The market as a linked chain*

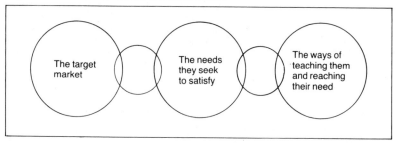

When the market is highly fragmented, like consumer markets, generalizations may be unavoidable. In industrial or government markets where a small number of key accounts exist, names should be attached and rigorous appraisals conducted.

To sum up

Segmentation and targeting has been done informally by most successful small firms throughout their existence. The associated techniques provide a structure for this and highlight new ways of identifying and bringing home new opportunities.

Spotting the sub-group against whom an initiative can be directed is only the first step. Matching this with a clear picture of how to reach them is the role of marketing research. Opening up the market calls for determined initiatives based on a thorough understanding of the wider forces in the market and the various complementary and conflicting forces.

Action Guidelines _____

1 List the features your customers have in common (other than that they buy from you).

_____

_____

_____

_____

_____

_____

2 Is there anything in this which significantly affects their choice of you as a supplier?

| Yes/No |

If YES, what?

_____

_____

_____

_____

_____

3 Name any other customers or customer groups with these features in common.

_____

_____

_____

_____

_____

4 Why don't they buy from you?

_____

_____

_____

_____

115

5 Can the market (in its widest sense) you service be broken down into more cohesive sub-groups?

Yes/No

If YES, detail these using the concepts of:
Geography _____

_____

_____

Demography _____

_____

_____

Industrial Sector _____

_____

_____

Usage _____

_____

_____

Psychology _____

_____

_____

6 State in very specific and precise terms the size and nature of the groups which emerge.

_____

_____

_____

_____

7 Using your own criteria for your markets and customers build up a marketing grid.

10

Coming to Terms with the Wider Environment

- Neither the company nor its customers exist in isolation.
- The wider environment has a direct and on-going impact on company prosperity.
- Managers should look upon their market as a multi-stage system rather than separate transactions or relationships.

Introduction and aims

The most common explanation of failure or poor performance in any company, but particularly in small firms, is the intervention of some outside, uncontrollable force. It might be a sudden change of fashion eliminating the need for suede splits in grips for ski sticks. It can be a drastic cut in local authority spending. Sometimes your customers find their customers changing their buying policy to your disadvantage. These might be descriptions of the harshness of a competitive ecomony. Equally, they could reflect a reluctance to accept that fashion changes, governments cut and customers vary in ways that we can understand and occasionally predict.

It is important to build up an awareness of these forces and the ways in which success can be achieved by using them. However it is not an appreciation of their separate roles which is important here but how together they affect the company and its relationships.

This includes a series of single steps going in the same direction. Most marketing transactions involve a number of linked steps.

The prosperity of a manufacturer of cooker or heating timers and controls is influenced as much by the purchasing policies of the Electricity and Gas Boards as is the retailer of cookers. However his scope for selling to them or influencing them in other ways is very restricted.

Suppliers can have a major effect on trading. In the polymer industries the giant chemicals companies, ICI, BP, Shell, have vast amounts of data on applications of materials, customer attitudes, product strengths and weaknesses. The raw material producers, machinery suppliers, even the sources of finance can often directly affect the viability of a firm and its marketing plans.

The wider, general environment

Four broad forces determine the character, nature and development of any market. These are:
- **The state of the ecomony**
- **The political situation**
- **The prevailing culture(s)**
- **The state of technology**

Such forces affect the national and international situation as well as conditions in a particular market. The results, however, can be very different. A rapid rise in energy prices can depress the overall economy but boost demand for wood-burning stoves or bicycles.

In appraising the influence of these forces, *general* and *specific* conditions should be separated. The short-term or long-term implications should be identified and assessed.

The economic influences range from such global questions as the level of economic development, for instance is the market *primitive, just starting to develop, rapidly developing* or *industrially mature*? These factors will determine the type of products bought, even the likely methods of payment. A primitive economy is likely to be seeking agricultural equipment and trying to pay in kind. An industrially mature economy will be looking for finished manufactured, probably consumer, products and paying in cash or credit.

Beyond these general issues, specific features of a national economy will influence trade. We've become depressingly familiar with balance of payments, interest rates, inflation, unemployment and price indexes. Surprisingly, few small firms build this information into their operations on any basis other than ad hoc reactions tainted by wishful thinking. Economic forecasts are widely published by bodies such as the London Business School and the National Institute of Economic and Social Research. The firm should try to identify key indications and link them to both its wider and narrower interests (see Figure 18).

Figure 18   *Indicators and links*

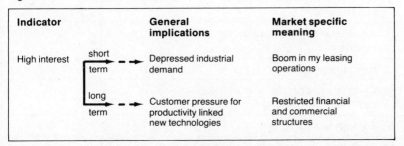

Indicator		General implications	Market specific meaning
High interest	short term	Depressed industrial demand	Boom in my leasing operations
	long term	Customer pressure for productivity linked new technologies	Restricted financial and commercial structures

This shows how a firm, once having identified an 'indicator', can work out the general implications and the specific mean for all or parts of its operations.

Once this type of analysis is embarked upon there is some tendency for indicators to multiply and there to be so many implications that no use is made of them. A small firm should seek to spot one, or at most, two such factors and review them regularly.

Political forces should be reviewed in precisely the same way. Most legislative action creates as many opportunities as threats, at least to those firms capitalizing on the refusal of others to accept its implications.

Technological change poses perhaps the greatest threats and opportunities for smaller firms. Few manufacturers can afford not to have some system of technology monitoring. In retailing and services the same pattern is rapidly emerging, with changes

119

directly affecting their operations. A technology monitoring system should be split between processes and products and involve at least an annual review of the sources listed in Figure 19, adapted for specific industries or services.

Figure 19 *Technology audit*

	Product	Process
1 Trade and technical press		
2 Industry conference reports		
3 Supplier appraisal		
4 Customer assessment		
5 Scientific and engineering literature		
6 Industry research association reports		
7 Key personal contacts		
8 Centres of specialist knowledge (for example universities)		
9 Foreign search		
10 Agencies, for example, British Technology Group		
11 Directories and new product newsletters		

This should be regularly completed for the firm's major products and processes.

Culture is both more pervasive and more difficult to pin down effectively. It can incorporate such factors as fashion changes. Although the pace of these can be predicted, in six-monthly cycles, the direction and nature is hard to gauge. At the same time, some movements can be discerned, such as the desire for more aesthetic appeal, even in engineered items where demands for higher service levels and insistence on more information are frequent. The battle to understand these forces is part of most modern managers' operations.

How does the environment affect you?

These general environmental forces seldom act directly on a market or a specific firm. They are usually translated into direct action by more specific groups such as the media, the banks and other finance institutions, and pressure groups such as trade associations. Just as they adapt and interpret these wider forces, so they are more tangible and easier to evaluate and respond to.

Small firm managers seldom have the time or inclination to investigate these groups. Unfortunately it means that the power wielded by the media and other interpreters seldom takes their needs into account. Managers should more actively pursue such forces and be more open and involved with the media and trade associations at a local level.

How to use the marketing system

This is the network of relationships which connects the firm to its market(s). In the case of smaller firms, the role of *suppliers* is particularly important, as they are a source of considerable potential support and assistance. The small firm manager has the great advantage of being a customer with the ability to press for specific help and assistance. The technical, financial and commercial capability of all potential sources of goods and services should be understood and used as appropriate.

Today most markets are characterized by stiff, even fierce *competition*. The firm with the clearest appreciation of its rivals is the company most likely to succeed against them. Despite that, it is remarkable how vague managers are in their assessments of competitors, their capabilities and the nature of the challenge posed.

In static markets (common enough today) the only source of added volume is business won from current competitors in existing markets or new ones in new markets. The marketing 'fact book' should include a thorough appraisal of all rivals, their customers and any scope for competitive advantage.

Most markets involve intermediaries who stand between the

121

company and the market or final user of its product. This intermediary can be a retailer, wholesaler, fabricator, assembler or user of services. Assessments need to match current value as a customer with a rigorous assessment of his competitive status. Component suppliers to British Leyland ought to have seen the erosion of their market long before the crisis of the late 1970s.

Occasionally this customer/intermediary assessment can lead to a shift in company strategy at an optimal time. It is usually easier to win a new client when the general market is strong than when the decline of a customer is so advanced that a crisis exists.

The end customers are as much your concern as his. Even when the firm has limited scope to influence their behaviour, as in the case of the controls firm noted earlier, knowledge can pay off. This has its most obvious benefit when the company can build into its offering assets enhancing the client's competitiveness. Occasionally this can mean second guessing. More often it means being keyed up to react quickly with major improvements in customer service.

To sum up

The small firm which survives and prospers today will be the one which matches traditional strengths in flexibility and creativity with breadth of vision. This means looking beyond its immediate market and seeking to understand and relate to the external forces determining its destiny. Be aware.

Simultaneously the market needs to be looked on in a different, more rigorous way, both as a network influenced by the forces discussed, and as a complex multi-stage structure of relationships. Success in converting this into positive managerial action provides the route to commercial prosperity.

Action Guidelines _____

1 Identify the key economic, cultural, political indicators:

		Indicator	General Implication	Specific Implication
Economic	(1)	_____	_____	_____
	(2)	_____	_____	_____
Cultural	(1)	_____	_____	_____
	(2)	_____	_____	_____
Political	(1)	_____	_____	_____
	(2)	_____	_____	_____

2 Complete the Technology Audit (see Page 120)

3 Complete supplier support appraisal:

Supplier	Technical	Financial	Commercial
(1) _____	_____	_____	_____
	_____	_____	_____
	_____	_____	_____
(2) _____	_____	_____	_____
	_____	_____	_____
	_____	_____	_____
(3) _____	_____	_____	_____
	_____	_____	_____
	_____	_____	_____

4 List *all* competitors:

_____

_____

_____

_____

_____

_____

5 Identify competitor based, business winning opportunities:

_____

_____

_____

6 Major Intermediary Appraisal

Intermediary	Strengths	Weaknesses	Opportunities	Threats
(1) _____	_____	_____	_____	_____
	_____	_____	_____	_____
	_____	_____	_____	_____
(2) _____	_____	_____	_____	_____
	_____	_____	_____	_____
	_____	_____	_____	_____
(3) _____	_____	_____	_____	_____
	_____	_____	_____	_____
	_____	_____	_____	_____
(4) _____	_____	_____	_____	_____
	_____	_____	_____	_____
	_____	_____	_____	_____

7 Identify the key feature of the end-user market:

_____

_____

_____

8 Draw up the firm's marketing system with threat points and opportunity points starred *.

Section 3

Marketing in Action

11
Taking Marketing Action

- Marketing strategies provide a summary of the ways the firm will seek to achieve its objectives.
- The strategy gives a common *language of action* to the firm, its management team and specific individuals.
- Strategies must be distinguished from tactics which are specifically linked to action.

Introduction and aims

In favourable market conditions it is possible for firms to survive, even prosper, with a passive attitude to the customers and the market. The company is in business and so is part of a network of relationships and has certain capabilities. Clients seek out its services more often than it looks for customers.

The changes in most markets over the last few years have seriously undermined this passive approach. Stay passive and the result can only be failure.

Successful small firms impose a clear sense of direction on their marketing effort by:
- offering customers something special or additional to simple responsiveness
- establishing their individual identity and value
- going out and working with their market

Often the crisis created by the drying up of demand prompts a furious spate of action and expenditure with little sense of real purpose or direction.

A small food producer in Yorkshire found major accounts declining. He decided to improve his image and quality while developing new delicatessen lines. At the same time he let his sales staff engage in widespread discounting. Customers found the combination of high quality image and extensive discounting difficult to accept. They felt that quality must be declining so rejected the new lines.

A marketing strategy is designed to draw these threads together.

There are two sides to any strategy:
1 Competitive advantage(s)
2 Internal controls

A strategy provides a framework for actions. The outward framework – the operational areas – is the scene for tactics. Tactics normally relate to particular actions, either directly, e.g. choosing a particular promotional technique, or indirectly, e.g. seeking to establish a specific image. Tactics should be geared to turn strategy into a series of actions. Consistency between strategy and tactics is essential.

Marketing strategy: various types

The importance of setting and persisting with objectives has been emphasized. This is particularly important when strategies are being evolved.

A number of methods of arriving at objectives for individuals, groups or organizations exist or have been developed:
• *Management by Extrapolation* This is based on the maxim 'If it was good enough last year, it's good enough today'. There are usually some trends in performance and, providing

these are going upwards, then everything is OK.

- *Management by Crisis*   No problem is so serious that it cannot be ignored until the last minute. This can be satisfying personally, as the trouble shooter or problem solver is often the boss, who again proves himself to be indispensable. It works until the number or scale of the crises overwhelms the firm.

- *Management by Hope (or Inspiration)*   Faced with a dynamic, changing or complex market, perhaps the best thing is to cross one's fingers and hope that either troubles will go away or that a single inspired idea will solve the problem. Many managers approach marketing with this in mind, expecting some magic trick to emerge to overcome adversity. Unfortunately this can prove both costly and debilitating. Costs grow as the firm is driven in a number of directions, led by ill thought out ideas and chance pressure.

- *Management by Objectives*   This calls upon the firm to state clearly its objectives. Separate departments identify their objectives in a clear and consistent way. These are constructively reviewed by all those involved.

  Managers of small firms are frequently wary of this. They worry about under-achievement and conservatism. Experience shows that if properly performed, based on discussion and dialogue – *not imposed* – the problem is the reverse. Managers tend to overstate their objectives.

The main warning is that the system of setting objectives has to be applied rigorously and throughout the firm. It should be clearly directed, well-organized and comprehensive or the results may be worse than if no objectives have been set.

The strategy exists to achieve the objectives. If it is to be implemented by others besides the author, it needs to be kept simple. A simple, implemented strategy is better than a complex, ignored strategy.

An invaluable way of looking at strategies is in terms of the match of markets/customers and products/services. The matrix below can be used to review alternatives.

Figure 20 *Marketing strategy matrix*

| Markets/ Customer | | Products/Services | |
		Existing	New
	Existing	'Penetration'	'Produce/Service development'
	New	'Market development'	'Diversification'

Each marketing strategy indicated has its strengths and weaknesses plus implications for specific actions.

A penetration strategy means fighting to improve the performance of current products or services in existing markets. Often the struggle is for improved market share. The products or services might be in the firm, but not applied in this market.

A steel stockholder benefited enormously by keeping his staff specializing in stainless steels fully informed on new mild steel-cutting facilities. This allowed them to spot opportunities for increasing the firm's share of the business of established customers.

More often this means looking for ways to improve market share. This requires that the market is clearly defined, the share closely watched and specific ways introduced and monitored to squeeze out a larger share. Price flexibility (not just cutting) and service level changes are critical here. Increasing market share is often the best route to short-term profit improvement.

Product/Service development   Although the detail of innovation and product development will be examined in Unit 14, the underlying strategy with its opportunities and attendant risks should be understood.

This calls for using one's knowledge of the market, its needs and quirks, to increase one's range of offerings (or to substitute for current products or services). There can be direct benefits as new products or services generate returns. Sometimes the wider pay-offs are more important, particularly when linked with a concerted search for improved productivity or new ways of making or processing the product or service. As the firm's 'range' widens new customers trying the innovations may convert to existing facilities.

Research into late night opening of garages and supermarkets in the US illustrates this. It was found that even when the turnover in the new 'unsocial' hours did not justify it, increases during the rest of the day more than paid for it. Customers expected the store to be open, got into the habit of going and didn't bother to look further. An experience of finding the shop, garage, restaurant, hotel, theatre, etc. closed, dramatically reduced their likelihood of trying it again (assuming alternatives existed).

Market development is probably the oldest marketing strategy geared to growth. The firm takes its current offerings to new markets or areas or countries. The scope here is enormous particularly where the firm's determination, expertise or technology gives it a competitive edge over those currently servicing the market.

There are many forms of this:

> A Scottish landowner had always rented part of his river for seasonal fishing. He decided to expand this to all the year fishing. He encouraged new customers from across Scotland to use his facilities.

> An engineering firm in the East Midlands pushed hard to win new customers in the West Midlands, Yorkshire and East Anglia.

> An artist craftsman who had always sold from his workshop had illustrations of his work accepted by the Crafts Advisory Council to interest retailers.

A willingness to adapt approaches and attitudes is essential here. A very small northern clothing maker might nervously face the challenge of a massive increase in turnover if major clothing retailers were to be serviced. A company used to working on commission might need to introduce its own designs.

Diversification This means going beyond existing markets *and* existing products into wholly new situations. These might be 'green field' situations where a gap has been left which the firm can fill. Occasionally business expertise developed in one area can be transferred to new areas. Unfortunately, fields that look green from a distance can often turn out to be swamps.

131

Success here usually means identification of something *unique* about the firm's expertise, technology, service or product, giving a real competitive edge. A rigorous appraisal, backed by a willingness to withdraw, is essential. Often problems emerge fairly early on but a variety of factors, notably pride and a reluctance to admit 'I'm wrong', drive the firm forward.

Choice The strategies described above are alternatives with different levels of risk and potential benefit. Even if they all seem to be good ideas, we should:

❝ improve our penetration of the current market, get new customers for old products, find new products for old customers and move into new areas. **❞**

A hard strategic choice should be made and followed through. Following all approaches gives little sense of direction while straining the limited resources of a small company.

Recognizing the different levels of risk can help in this choice. Risk gets greater as the company moves into increasingly unfamiliar territory.

Figure 21 *Shifting risks in strategy*

| | | Products/Services | |
		Existing	New
Markets/ Customers	Existing	Low risk	Medium risk
	New	Medium risk	High risk

Likelihood of failure increases as novelty of situation increases with a new product *and* a new market.

Sometimes the greater risks are matched by scale of opportunity. Only where this is the case or the implications are fully appreciated, should a small firm adopt this policy.

Although no hard and fast rules can be put forward, the most favoured strategies are likely to be:
- Penetration
- Market Development

- Product/Service Development
- Diversification

The selection of strategy should be based on the type of audit and analysis discussed earlier.

Once the strategic alternative has been chosen, the operational strategy within which policies will emerge needs to be designed. It is difficult to do this effectively if alternatives are not identified and their differential advantages fully understood.

Strategic issues

Once the strategic alternatives have been sifted, the firm ought to be in a position to embark on the three next steps.

Three steps:
- a Problems Appraisal
- a Structured Review
- an Analysis of Alternatives

The problems appraisal This should be a free-flowing analysis of the practical meaning of the strategy chosen. In particular the barriers to achievement should be identified. This is best done through a 'brainstorming' session with as many interested parties involved as possible.

Figure 22   *The problem appraisal matrix*

		Control	
		Easy	Difficult
Significance	High		
	Low		

The structured review A strategy worksheet can greatly facilitate this.

It should incorporate:

- The Challenges in rank order
- Business Decision Areas related to these
- Strategies open for tackling them
- Implications for other aspects of the firm
- Costs and Profits

At this stage avoid clichés about 'better' service, 'high' quality. It can help to ask 'What is so special or unique about our offering that would encourage an established customer of a competitor to change?' A positive answer should be checked or tested rather than merely accepted.

The strategy chosen should be stated in a clear summary form of no more than 50 to 60 words.

Analysing alternatives   Most marketing situations can be tackled in a variety of ways. Without going into the detail above, the more obvious alternatives should be noted and summarized. The firm should then embark on a critique of the alternatives.

This examination of alternatives may lead the firm to re-examine the strategy chosen. This should be done willingly. It is better to resolve difficulties here than in the market.

Tactics

The essential feature of a marketing tactic is that it is operational and implies clearly defined action. Spheres of tactical action include market selection, products and product mix, advertising, sales and promotion, distribution and prices. Together these turn the strategy into action. The marketing strategy has little meaning outside these programmes. The customer has only these clues to build up his picture of whether the firm and its offerings are truly for him.

The strategy provides the ground rules within which the tactics will emerge. Consistency between tactics and strategy will provide a corporate sense of purpose.

Much of the rest of this book concentrates on the nature and form of the features making up these tactics. The style of coverage will be very different from the foregoing discussion. Performance is the key. No firm will reap the benefits if it misses the essential links between thought and action.

To sum up

Many forces combine to increase awareness of the importance of marketing strategies. In a changing situation these will supply consistent reference points for policies. By doing this, the firm is directing its efforts, not putting itself into a strait-jacket. However, once chosen, the strategy should be executed, not shelved until an excuse is needed for failure.

Action Guidelines ━━━━━━━━

1 Which of the following describes the best method of setting objectives?

Management by Extrapolation ☐

Management by Crisis ☐

Management by Hope ☐

Management by Objectives ☐

Other (detail) _____ ☐

_____

_____

2 Describe how this is used.

_____

_____

3 Ask each senior executive (including self) to state:

	Executive A	*Executive B*	*Executive C*
The Firm's Marketing Objectives	_____	_____	_____
	_____	_____	_____
	_____	_____	_____
	_____	_____	_____
His/her own Marketing Related	_____	_____	_____
	_____	_____	_____
	_____	_____	_____
	_____	_____	_____

4 Review this, noting in particular their consistency.

_____

_____

_____

5 Using the Marketing Strategy Matrix, indicate where current policies are directed.

| | Products/Services | |
	Existing	New
Markets/Customers Existing		
New		

6 Using the matrix, select from the alternatives.

7 Complete the Strategy Worksheet:

XYZ Company – 198–

Problems   (1) _____   (3) _____
(2) _____   (4) _____

Decision areas	Strategies open	Costs and returns	Integration

8 Summarize the strategy:

_____

_____

_____

9 List and review alternatives:

Costs	Strategies	Conditions

12

A Total Product/
Service Proposition

- Customers usually seek to satisfy a number of needs when purchasing, hiring or leasing a product or service.

- Firms which think only in terms of the product or service and its specifications will gradually find their prices eroded as others learn to match these.

- Intangible attributes are often sought by customers. These are frequently inexpensive to introduce and difficult to copy.

Introduction and aims

The words 'product' and 'service' pose special problems for those engaged in building up profitable sales. Their use misleads and does a disservice to producers and suppliers. Both conjure up an image of something which is free-standing, capable of being separated from its context, an individual physical good. Nothing is further from the truth.

This view owes much to the perspectives of nineteenth century economists. They viewed markets in terms of a collection of separate but indistinguishable products – Canadian grain is allegedly the same as US grain. The best way to sell this type of item is for the producers to bring it to auction where a large number of buyers would bid. Eventually, supply and demand would meet and the economic price would be reached.

Even in the last century this was a poor image of reality. Clipper ships raced to be the first to the market – gaining premium prices for high service levels. Canadian grain was easier to mill, so worth more to some customers. French wines had a reputation which won higher prices from those able to pay. Repeatedly it was shown that when the customer could choose, he exercised his discretion. The product plus the service was paid for. The full costs of using various alternatives were borne in mind. A purchase transaction is not a mechanical act.

The notion of the *total product proposition* brings this to the fore. It emphasizes the transaction entered into by the customer, not merely the item offered by the supplier. It is easy to lose sight of the roundness of the customer's view when our attention is focused on the physical product or service.

Buyers want:
- the right product or service
- at the right time
- in an acceptable condition
- at an 'affordable' cost
- it to be introduced in a way that makes for awareness of the total product proposition and its relevance.

None of these features can be treated in isolation. Together they form the **total product proposition**.

The firm that cannot state its total product proposition does not know its product or service. Without product knowledge (including services), most sales efforts will be a struggle.

Here the implications of this approach to the company's offering are explored. Ways of building up a total product proposition are described with special emphasis on the interrelationships involved.

The marketing mix

In designing a total product proposition, the firm has at its disposal a number of features of marketing effort that can be controlled. These can be mixed in a variety of ways to suit the needs of different target markets or segments.

Success depends on the match of mix and market.

The controllable marketing variables that the firm has at its disposal can be broadly divided into – Product or Service, Price, Distribution and Promotion. Their combination or, more accurately, the mixing of their different and diverse features constitute the firm's offering.

Figure 23   *The marketing mix*

Product/ Service	Price	Distribution	Promotion
Quality	List(s)	Number and types	Advertising
Design	Discounting	of middlemen	Merchandising
Features	Trade-ins	Density	Sales support
Options	Credit	Availability	Promotional
Tailoring	Payment terms	Location	support
Style	Financing	Customer search	Press relations
Name		time	Public relations
Packaging		Warehousing	Exhibitions
Ranges		Stock levels	Trade shows
Sizes		Delivery time	Seminars
Support		Method of	Conferences
services		delivery	
Warranty			
Trade-in			
Returns			

The mix should be specifically designed with a particular customer or group in mind. This leads to some 'natural' mixes.

A specialized marketing consultancy service may mix: high quality services, tailored to customer requirements, with high prices, restricted credit, limited availability, selective exposure and frequent use of conferences and seminars. These would be organized to reach a restricted client list made up of blue chip companies willing to pay well for strategic advice.

A manufacturer of industrial fasteners might mix: large volume production, a wide selection, long credit, elimination of middlemen, rapid delivery, high stocks, with low prices, extensive use of personal selling and some exhibition work, to reach major original equipment manufacturers based locally but able to buy world-wide.

The mix should be reviewed in terms of:

- Internal consistency
- Appeal to identifiable customer groups
- Uniqueness

The company mission

This *total product* or *service proposition* should be summarized into a brief statement sometimes described as a company mission. This builds the bridge between the firm and the customer.

One firm recently summarized its mission as 'becoming the BMW of the office equipment world'. This conveyed a picture of first rate engineered products with a high quality and prestige image combining to justify premium prices and high status.

Products, offerings and services This type of discussion is equally relevant whether the company is in manufacturing, trading or services. Many of the terms may need to be redefined but the importance of a total proposition persists.

In the service sector companies often build in additional features whose intangible nature can lead to a reluctance to charge properly for them. These can range from account management, to detailed commercial back-up, to time consuming pre-project development. These should be clearly specified in the proposition in order for the full implications to be worked out with the costs and benefits fully appraised.

To sum up

The notion of a total offering or total product proposition is essential if:

141

- the diverse nature of the market(s) chosen, and
- the scope for real differentiation made possible by technology, new facilities and services, etc.

are to be fully exploited.

Ultimately the design of a total product proposition or working marketing mix is a *creative, not a mechanical act.* This emphasizes the significance of arriving at a **totality** not a hotchpotch of separate features.

Action Guidelines _____

1 Against what group(s) are the firm's offerings targeted?

_____

_____

_____

2 What features identify this group and separate it from the wider market?

_____

_____

_____

3 Detail the total proposition sought by the group in terms of the mix variables.

Product _____

_____

_____

Price _____

_____

_____

Promotion _____

_____

_____

Distribution _____

_____

_____

4 How would this be summarized into an embracing statement of total product proposition?

_____

_____

5 What is unique or special about this – **in the eyes of the target market?**

_____

_____

_____

13

Managing the Existing Products and Services

- The firm's product, production process or service is the core around which the rest of the firm's marketing efforts are built.
- Products or services are usually made up of bundles of attributes of varying importance to the customer.
- This generates the wealth from which all other company developments emerge.

Introduction and aims

Until recently there was a curiously casual approach to the products and services currently offered by firms. Although they generated the wealth for the firm, there was a sense that there was little one could do today about today's offerings. The income produced could be used for future developments but the product itself was fixed and unchanging. In smaller companies the diversity of offering, the extent of 'customizing' and the importance of flexibility means that managing existing products and services is the key to the firm's future.

Single product or service firms are rare creatures. Even when the basic commodity is the same – industrial fasteners, hand tools, money, consultancy – the way the firm has adapted and developed its range can produce immense diversity. A self-employed consultant able to advise effectively on a large number of discrete taxation and financial problems is fairly normal. Success in managing these diverse offerings will play a major part in the firm's prosperity. In process industries, such as plastics and engineering, the firm's technology and specialized expertise is the basis of its business, as they make to customer specifications. Variety is the norm. Ability to get the best from this will separate the failures, marginals and successes amongst firms.

Today there is the increasing emphasis on 'service' support even in traditional manufacturing industries. Let's look at the practical implications and a way of managing them.

Product: attributes and increments

Most of us entering a transaction give little real attention to what the buyer is really buying. The nature of the firm's basic product can easily be obscured as time, new acquisitions and a variety of changes add new features to the firm's operations.

The advertising industry illustrates this type of development. Once the ad-agency was merely the media owner's sales agent. He sold space and claimed a commission. Eventually an enterprising ad man spotted an opportunity to gain a march on his rivals by giving advice and assistance in areas such as copy and illustrations. Competition raised the stakes here as clients spent more and expected more. Soon, other advertising entrepreneurs won accounts by providing market research support, assistance in planning and the plethora of added services characteristic of the advertising business. Now companies are looking back, spotting particular services and specializing in them. The media buying agency, the creative 'hot-shop', has emerged as services are pruned and clients are given the choice between full service agencies and specialists.

This pattern of incremental development around a basic offering is very common. However, these additions can slowly move the firm away from its specialism or simply make it blind to the core around which all else has been built. A company serious about understanding itself must identify and comprehend its basic product.

This analysis should start in terms of customer benefit sought, *not* product attributes. In essence this is the primary reason why our customers buy *our product* – what problem are they solving, need are they meeting or benefit are they seeking? At the same time ask why they buy it *from us*. These issues should be kept separate at this stage.

145

Once the basic benefits are identified, the basic product or service – stripped of packaging, name, styling, etc. – can be determined. In many cases it will no longer be offered by the firm in this form. This is not a problem but it may mean that the nature of the business should be redefined to reflect this revised basic service or product.

This core requires a visible or tangible form. The *formal product* provides this. This incorporates those features of styling, packaging, quality level, special features and naming introduced to confer special benefits and achieve a tangible pay-off. Each facet of the formal product needs to be diagnosed and the trade benefits fully understood. This is particularly true if costs are involved or modifications planned.

Value analysis is at the centre of this. Any product cost should provide a commercial benefit. Often features have been introduced in the past to meet particular needs. The need has gone but the feature remains incorporated.

Besides these direct, formal product characteristics, many small firms *augment* their offering through warranties, free delivery and installation, back-up services, etc. The costs and pay-offs here should be monitored.

Throughout this process the most common problem for small firms is *product* or *service drift*. This drift is the process by which product features or attributes are added which tie up resources but where no attempt has been made to assess the commercial returns. Drift can seriously erode profits. It can produce *product clutter* as features compete for customer attention, or new developments are rejected because there is already too much on offer.

The product line

Most small firms offer a number of items or services to customers. These constitute the company's product line. Ideally these will contribute to each other in ways which are greater than the sum of the individual parts.

Each service or product offered in a line should be reviewed in terms of both its individual value and its impact on others.

146

An efficient firm will keep the following points constantly in mind:

1 *Product risk* An existing offering or new idea might put other products or services at risk to no great advantage.

2 *Product benefit* The scope for mutual support should be reviewed.
- Can customers be induced to buy the range?
- Can mutually supportive displays in stores, etc. increase impact and sales?

3 *Product elimination* One of the most effective ways of increasing short-term and medium-term profits is through appraisals of the current commercial viability of individual items in the range. Even when sales have virtually disappeared, companies will stick to products and services in the mistaken belief that 'nothing is lost'. But costs are incurred, even in services, when dead wood is retained.

A company seeking to develop its product range has available a number of methods of analysis.

A useful way of reviewing products and offerings is in terms of the markets served and positions in the market (note the earlier discussion on defining a market).

Figure 24 *Four-cell product matrix*

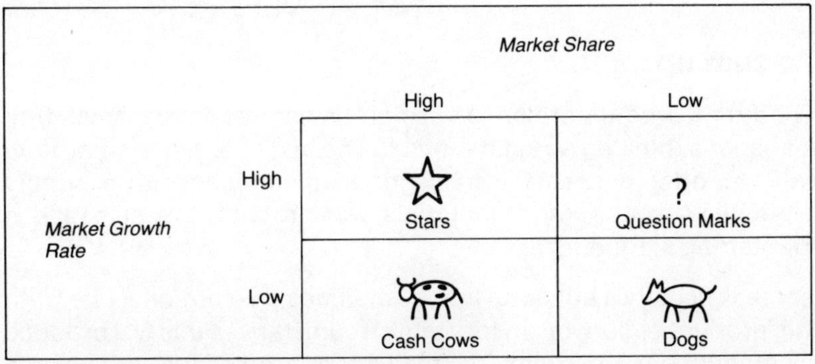

The use of the four-cell product matrix allows the firm to examine its product range. It analyses each type of offering in terms of the criteria set.

Product A ('Star') is in a high growth market, such as personal computers, and the firm has a high market share. This has substantial potential for returns but is likely to put resources under pressure as the challenge to hold share during rapid growth is faced.

Product B ('Cash cow') is in a low growth market but the firm has a high market share. Here current returns are likely to be good but long term potential is limited. Cash is generated but has to be effectively invested for the firm's future.

Product C ('Question mark') is in a high growth market but the company's share is low. The pressure on resources will be great as the company tries to keep up but the current returns may be low. The long term potential is doubtful as there is a weak business base.

Product D ('Dog') combines low growth with low market share. These contribute little currently and show little scope for improvement but can consume considerable scarce resources.

Effective use of the matrix involves combining this analysis with management action to move towards substantial current income and long term growth. Allocating the different products and services offered by the firm in these terms will give a picture of the balance of the firm's activities, likely opportunities and potential threats.

To sum up

The firm's product or service lies at the centre of most small firm manager's thinking about their firm. The ability to make some item well, to offer a special service or to meet requests to supply particular components or materials, was probably the main reason for starting up the firm.

There is usually a powerful link, sometimes an emotional one, with this product or service. In the right circumstances this will produce a commitment to quality, a creativity and a product knowledge unmatched in the larger firm. Under the wrong conditions it produces a reluctance to think hard and rigorously that will undermine the firm's operations.

Action Guidelines ————————

1 Identify the core benefit sought by the different groups of customers served:

_____

_____

2 Describe the firm's core product(s):

_____

_____

3 List the key formal product attributes and their related customer pay-offs.

Attributes   *Pay-offs*

_____   _____

_____   _____

_____   _____

_____   _____

4 Describe the results of any *value analysis* conducted recently.

_____

_____

5 What results have emerged from a review of:

(1) Product Risk(s)? _____

_____

(2) Product Benefit(s)? _____

_____

(3) Opportunities for Product Elimination? _____

_____

6 Complete the Four-Cell Product Matrix for the firm's products and services.

	Market Share	
	High	*Low*
Market Growth Rate — *High*		
Low		

14

Innovation and New Product/Service Development

- Change is endemic.
- The firm which hopes to prosper in the medium to long term will only do so if it continually innovates and adapts.
- Innovation involves risks which can only be controlled through a structured and disciplined approach to its management.

Introduction and aims

In the late 1970s a major government report on 'Industrial Innovation' (the ACARD report) argued that a major reason for Britain's industrial decline lay in its poor performance in innovation. The report emphasized the distinction between the two *separate* activities of invention and innovation.

Invention with its emphasis on newness, novelty and creativity is a field in which Britain excels. Unfortunately it has no direct links with commercial success. A project can be brilliantly inventive but show no meaningful returns.

Innovation emphasizes this commercial return. There is no need for the idea to be wholly new. It can be transferred from elsewhere. It can even be a return to a traditional offering. The key lies in its introduction for the first time to a particular market.

Here, the different forms of innovation will be described with their risks and potential pay-offs reviewed. The sources of ideas are described with particular emphasis on low cost, minimum risk routes.

The small firm seeking to benefit from this discussion must realize that this analysis can only be separated from earlier sections in a fairly arbitrary way. A programme of activities should be planned and executed in conjunction with wider marketing developments.

The nature of innovation

In order to understand the role and potential contribution of innovation to the firm, it is worthwhile recognizing the four different forms it takes.

Forms of innovation:
- The improvement and development of existing offerings or products
- The improvement and development of existing processes
- The introduction of new production processes
- The introduction of new products or services

Despite the tendency to think largely in terms of the last of these, in all probability the small firm will find the others both more practical and more profitable. Despite the appeal of the new product, any programme of activity should lean strongly towards these alternatives.

Successful innovation in all these areas is founded on two basic principles: the generation of a stock of creative ideas for product or process development or innovation, and their rigorous and careful evaluation and selection. The probability of failure with a new product or service is high, particularly under the following conditions:

1 The firm is entering a new market with an untested product.
2 There is neither a price nor a major product advantage.

A useful way of looking at this is in terms of a generation and screening process.

Figure 25 *The generation and selection system*

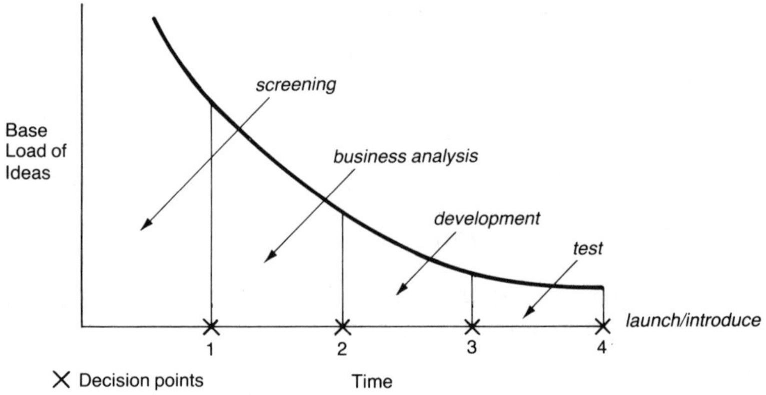

Although this may seem fairly self-evident to many managers, the need to make carefully judged decisions at specific points is often ignored. It is essential to do this. The corollary to a meaningful decision – the will to say 'No' – is regularly ignored in the hope that something will turn up.

Innovation demonstrates 'Murphy's Law' – if something can go wrong, it will.

Generating ideas

There are many sources of new ideas for improving the production process, adaptation or new products or services. These include:

Market research	Foreign search
Market gap analysis	Study of use
Technological developments	Leads from suppliers
Brainstorming	Internal research and
Customer comments	development
Introduction of design features	Individual insight

A particularly useful avenue for the small firm is foreign search. Britain is one of the few net exporters of patents and licences.

Although this partly reflects national creativity and inventiveness, one element is undoubtedly a reluctance to take up the licences and agencies on offer from abroad. A company reviewing the need to extend its range of products or services is well advised to explore the scope to import or take up an agency – if only to try out fully the idea or its application.

Implementation and introduction

A market-place orientation is critical to successful innovation and new product/service development. Changes should be judged in terms of their value to the customer or client, not some internal reasons or justifications. (These should provide controls, not directions.)

Often it will emerge that a relatively simple improvement, perhaps making the product easier to store, easier to use or lower in price, will reap the real marketing benefits.

In the food market, the St Ivel 'Five Pints' packaging change has proved to be one of the more successful recent innovations. St Ivel were attempting to break into the dried milk market. This was dominated by Cadbury's 'Marvel' and a number of own label brands. The market power of the former allowed them to spend heavily on advertising. The retailer own label brands were significantly cheaper. St Ivel broke into the market by introducing a plastic bottle containing the dried equivalent of five pints of milk. This appealed to many customers who preferred it to the tins used by their rivals. They saw it as being far closer to the traditional bottle of milk.

Where big changes and large scale improvements are involved, 'Poisoned Apple Marketing' is worth cultivating. Here the small firm capitalizes on its speed of reaction. Other firms' efforts are watched as they introduce new products. Their errors are examined and avoided and, with speed on the company's side, the market can be scooped by an improved offering.

A common criticism of small firm innovation is directed at the poor reliability and low quality of early batches. The introductory period will largely determine the long-term potential.

153

Avoid being someone else's 'poisoned apple'!

To sum up

Despite the risks, innovation and new product or service development is essential in seeking to continue operations today. The risks can be reduced with a programmed, planned and disciplined approach. Unfortunately, risks can never be entirely eliminated.

Action Guidelines _____

1 Opportunity Checklist
   (a) Improvement and development of existing products and
       services. _____
       _____
       _____
       _____
       _____
       _____
       _____

   (b) Improvement and development of existing process of production
       or managing services. _____
       _____
       _____
       _____
       _____
       _____
       _____

   (c) Introduction of new production processes. _____
       _____
       _____
       _____
       _____
       _____
       _____

   (d) Introduction of new products. _____
       _____
       _____
       _____
       _____
       _____
       _____

15

Price

- **Prices are part of the marketing mix, not separate from or an alternative to it.**
- **Alternative pricing strategies can be identified and executed.**
- **Prices should be geared to specific goals.**

Introduction and aims

Most managers see price as the centre of their relationship with their customers. The phrase 'it all comes down to price' is seldom far from their lips. Although this may describe reality, it need not always be the case.

This view of price seldom acknowledges the complexity of the price decision. Although price can be readily defined as:

❝ the amount for which a product, service or idea is exchanged **❞**

it contains many features which can affect the precise amount paid, the real cost to the buyer and the true income for the supplier.

Here a rather different notion of price is introduced. It is a complex and manipulable feature of a marketing mix. The diversity of the price decision will be emphasized. At the same time, its role as the most powerful and sensitive instrument of marketing policy, at a tactical level, is also stressed.

Understanding prices

In small firms decisions about prices generally have a significance far greater than for larger companies. The resources may not exist to spend on advertising to improve images or enhance loyalty. Brand or company identity will be less well established. The customer may be less aware of distinguishing features of the offering or more conscious of rivals.

This situation is made worse for many firms supplying industrial and commercial customers on a contract or tender basis. The specifications are tightly defined, the search for alternatives is wide and the buyers are professional. Pricing policies can end up revolving around a constant battle to keep prices as low as possible to keep volume business, without which the firm would fail.

It would be foolish to pretend that this is not the situation facing many small firms. This is virtually a commodity marketing situation. There is little that can be done quickly to reverse this situation. Longer term policies do exist.

Prices involve payments. The *true* price obtained reflects promptness of payment and restricted credit as much as the amount charged. Alongside the price level, the credit given is perhaps the most important *decision* area. Regrettably the notion of a decision is easily lost as credit is demanded or payment problems grow. *Here the firm must stop, take stock and impose immediate and ruthless marketing controls.*

Inefficiency in invoicing and monthly statements is common. Prompt personal follow-up is the most practical way of speeding up payment. This can mean the chief executive intervening directly to arrive at a settlement or method of settlement.

Often the absolute price level may be far less important than the collection. Prompt invoicing is worth £s.

The diversity of price

Prices should not be set first and separately, with the discussion of discounts or allowances following. These require simultaneous decisions. Discounts, the use of financial services, credit and trade-ins have direct costs for the supplier. Concessions here should be reflected in the price arrived at.

157

Price goals

Prices, like all other marketing tactics, should be directly linked to the goals, strategies and wider objectives set. Over time, different pricing policies should be linked with alternative goals.

Among the goals open to the firm are:

- *Volume Increases*   A price designed primarily to build volume ought to recognize that this will involve some cost. This cost will be met through lower prices.

- *Protecting the Business*   This is a difficult policy to execute solely through price, as the type of loyalty often involved is generally linked to images of the firm, technical abilities, etc. The pricing programme will generally involve establishing 'entry forestalling prices', pitching a price level capable of giving a reasonable return but not high enough to encourage others to invest in opening up the market.

- *Profit Maximizing*   Typically this calls for considerable selectivity between customer groups. Buyers are chosen in terms of their willingness to pay high prices. Volume will be cut rather than prices reduced.

- *Revenue Build-up*   The owner needs to be in a position to establish precisely how much additional income will come and how much additional expenditure will be incurred on each sale.

Action in all these areas calls for systematic information gathering. This will build up a picture of the market and the likely reaction among customers and competitors to price changes.

The close links that many managers of small firms have with their clients and customers is an asset here. Buyers are surprisingly helpful when approached directly. However, the information gathering should be cross-checked with more objective measures.

Cost based approaches to price

Inherent in the idea of a fair price is the concept of a reasonable return on the firm's investment and for its efforts. The firm is seeking to recoup its costs while generating wealth for its future.

The most common approach to cost based pricing, particularly in retailing, is **mark-up pricing**. Here a pre-determined percentage is added to established costs and a final price arrived at. Although this may seem straightforward, significant problems exist.

For manufacturers the challenge often lies in defining the attributable costs, particularly where some element of investment in future trading is involved.

For the service sector the nature of the cost poses special problems, given the intangible and personal nature of the offering being priced.

Flat percentages can be fatal particularly when they become entrenched over time.

A distributor of animal feedstuffs in the Highlands of Scotland added a fixed 15 per cent. High interest rates and slow payment meant that during 1981 and 1982 almost half this percentage was absorbed in servicing his debts. Another retailer worked on a single

Figure 26   *Breakeven chart*

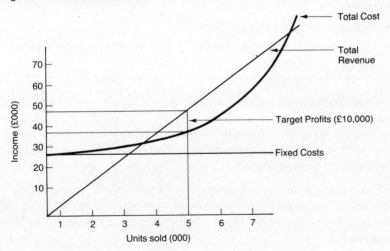

rate for all his products. He failed to realize that some lines had high wastage rates and others virtually none.

Target pricing based on breakeven analysis overcomes some of the problems faced by manufacturers in cost plus pricing. Here a breakeven chart is drawn up (see Figure 26). The likely sales volume is forecast, as are costs, and a target return on investment. The price which maximizes profits is chosen.

The flaw in target pricing using breakeven analysis brings out the fundamental weakness in cost based pricing:
- The price charged has a direct effect on demand – the factor being used to establish the price.

Market orientated prices

This approach seeks to redress the imbalance caused by the cost based view. Attitudes of buyers are established and likely demands based on possible prices arrived at.

In applying this approach failure to obtain an acceptable price can lead to:
- Abandonment of the product.
- Re-examination of the Marketing Mix variables to arrive at a new proposition.

Demand orientated pricing can lead to spectacular break-throughs, particularly in 'green field' situations. However, the routes to gathering data and the role of cost as a constraint on flexibility, rather than the factor that primarily determines prices, should be recognized and accepted.

Cost controls are as important in market based pricing as cost prices. The system of control is particularly important, as slackness can emerge which sometimes erodes the viability of the exercise.

Promotional prices and discounts

The flexibility of price as a marketing tool is amply demonstrated in its use for promotional development. Short-term price cuts do not seem to erode the quality reputation of the product in the way longer term reduction can. At the same time, even sophisticated buyers will respond favourably to a well designed price deal.

The legal context to price

To some degree complete freedom of action on prices is a thing of the past. Prices and pricing policies are subject to increasing scrutiny by government and other agencies.

The small firm will need to be aware of the actions of bodies such as the Office of Fair Trading and the Monopolies and Mergers Commission.

In particular sectors, notably health and defence, government takes a very interventionist role.

Perhaps more importantly, today laws exist on labelling, descriptions of price and the price conditions which can be imposed on customers and intermediaries. In this, the European Commission is playing an increasing role.

To sum up

Despite the importance given to pricing by small firm managers, there is relatively little awareness of its nature and potential as a subtle as well as powerful marketing tool. The temptation is always to take a uniform approach regardless of conditions. Here two features of the market can hold the key to success. In some cases low overheads will allow the firm to cut prices constantly with virtually all income making a meaningful contribution to the business. In other cases the firm understands its marginal costs and prices additional sales to cover these marginal costs.

This involves varying prices to meet marketing conditions. A new market may be willing to pay high prices for a line which is sold cheaply elsewhere. Time can play a part, discounts can encourage some customers to buy out of season.

Action Guidelines _____

1 For the firm's leading offerings, list the current prices of leading
   competitors.

	Item	Own Price	Rival A	Rival B	Rival C
(a)	_____	_____	_____	_____	_____
(b)	_____	_____	_____	_____	_____
(c)	_____	_____	_____	_____	_____
(d)	_____	_____	_____	_____	_____
(e)	_____	_____	_____	_____	_____

2 What is the true price mix offer for the major offering(s) or leading
   customer(s)?

_____

_____

_____

_____

_____

_____

3 Which Pricing Goals are set and how is it reflected in action?

Volume _____

Protection _____

Profit _____

Revenue _____

If more than one is used, in the case of separate products, indicate
which. These goals are mutually exclusive in the case of industrial
products or services.

162

16

Sell the Sizzle Not the Sausage

- Promotional activity is the visible part of marketing.
- Communication lies at the core of most promotional policy making.

Introduction and aims

Most managers view advertising, merchandising, press relations and sales force activity as separate, operationally independent factors in the firm's marketing efforts.

In practice, all are involved in communication about the firm and its products or services in some way. Each area will gain maximum benefits when complemented by activity in other areas of the promotional mix. This is illustrated by the old story of the salesman who arrived in the buyer's office to be told:

❛ I don't know who you are.
I don't know your company.
I don't know your company's product.
I don't know what your company stands for.
I don't know your company's customers.
I don't know your company's record.
I don't know your company's reputation.

Now, what was it you wanted to sell me?

The problem is serious for the large firm. For a small company, the name, even the reputation, may carry no greater weight without advertising back-up. Despite that, firms persist in sending sales staff out without literature or any preparation. The monetary saving is trivial against the potential time (and cost) of the individual salesman briefing the client.

A South coast firm specializing in storage equipment and shelf racking has sent its salesman to the Middle East every six months. However, it refused to reprint its brochures in Arabic or provide any sales aids like a tape slide presentation. The result was that each visit was almost a new exercise in prospecting rather than progress towards real sales.

Developing an effective promotional policy means recognizing and managing the relationships. The *communication* approach emphasizes the importance of using the promotional resources at the firm's command to present a consistent and effective message to the client.

Communication

It is possible to exist at the edge of a market, watching others gain handsome returns while languishing in the doldrums (even despite a better product or service). This problem is typically one of communication and awareness.

The complexity of promotional communication can prompt some managers to take a negative or idiosyncratic view of their promotional activities, never building them into their overall programmes. It is more useful to seek ways of cutting through these difficulties by developing a model or structure within which attempts to reach customers and clients can be assessed. A useful approach to this with relevance in all promotional activity is AIDA. This describes the stages through which the customer moves as he/she shifts from unawareness to purchase.

AIDA: An approach to assessing advertising
- **A**wareness
- **I**nterest
- **D**esire
- **A**ction

This is more useful in assessing particular promotional initiatives than in generating new ideas or aids. The sales promotion, the exhibition, the advertising, etc. can be judged in terms of how each contributes to the client's move through these pre-purchase stages.

The recipient of a promotional activity or communication is not a sponge, drawing upon the message but not affecting it. A view of this process should acknowledge the understanding, interpreting and responding aspects. (See Figure 27)

Figure 27   *Communication process*

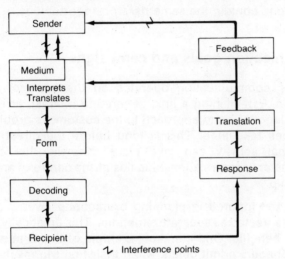

This model demonstrates how the sender passes his message through a medium to a potential customer. This can be the manufacturer placing his ad in a newspaper or magazine. The status and reputation of the medium affects the message, partly by requiring it to be put in a particular form, partly by having a more general impact on the impression gained by readers. This can range from enhancement, because the reader likes or respects the medium, to detriment, because of poor placing or bad reproduction. There is feedback to the advertiser when he reads or views the message. At the same time it is transmitted to the target market. Again there is a process of interpretation and understanding of the message. Unless this process is understood and the scope for interference or misunderstanding appreciated, the benefits of promotion will seldom be fully realized.

The medium and the message

The medium or vehicle used for promotion affects the nature of the message received. The same detail, reaction or interpretation cannot be handled by all forms. The salesman can communicate considerable detail, but in a highly interpretative and individual way. The salesman will be able to respond but this can distort the message, perhaps positively, at times negatively. Brochures and adverts don't contain the same risks or opportunities.

Communication goals and campaigns

Very little communication operates on the basis of a single interaction. Establishing a link, generating interest, arriving at a common language and approach to the customer's problems and needs does take time. This is long before the direct sales or promotional activity can take place. Knowing the customer through established relationships lies at the centre of any selling relationship.

This is often ignored in planning promotions. Events or trans-actions are treated as separate situations. This drastically reduces the likely benefits. One common example of this is in exporting where managers admit defeat when their first trip meets with no success. A campaigning approach, bringing together the various elements into a concerted thrust, will improve returns and generally cost less than an ill co-ordinated effort. A factor in this is the decay effect of actions here – the impact of an exhibition or of a newspaper article about the firm declines with time. Unless this is recognized, the 'window of opportunity' for the follow-up or support activity is lost.

Figure 28 illustrates the importance of the follow-up. When it is organized before the interest drops below the 'threshold', there is a progressive and real improvement betweeen visits or contacts. Once it drops below the threshold, a subsequent action means

Figure 28 *Promotional 'windows of opportunity'*

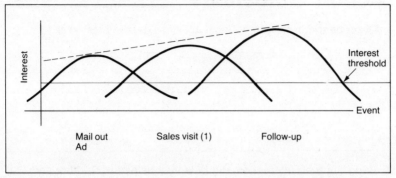

starting from scratch – that is, the window of opportunity closes below this threshold.

The promotional campaign and mix need to be goal related for three important reasons. In order to:

- provide criteria for evaluation
- supply a clear sense of direction
- capitalize on the considerable scope for internal substitutability, as between forms of promotion, and external substitutability.

To sum up

All firms are in the communications business. Information about their existence, their capabilities, their strengths, must be transmitted if the customer is to have the opportunity to respond.

One of the most profitable first steps for a small firm in this area can simply be to 'remind' people that the firm exists. It should never be assumed that physical proximity, even a tradition of trading together, eliminates the need to inform the buyer and keep him in touch.

In this context a campaigning approach based on making sure the promotional activities work together pays massive dividends. Piecemeal promotion is often worse than no promotion.

167

Action Guidelines _____

1 Describe the firm's promotional activities over the last year.

_____

_____

_____

_____

_____

_____

2 Bring out their interaction and how they helped each other and
operated as a concerted campaign.

_____

_____

_____

_____

_____

_____

3 What goals were set?
   (1) _____
   (2) _____
   (3) _____
   (4) _____

4 Promotional checklist
   How do current activities contribute to effective communication?

Stage	Activity A	Activity B	Activity C
Awareness	_____	_____	_____
Interest	_____	_____	_____
Desire	_____	_____	_____
Action	_____	_____	_____

5 Are any stages missed out? | Yes/No |

If YES, how does communication take place? _____

_____

_____

_____

_____

_____

6 Using the approach in Figure 27, draw up the firm's communication process, indicating interference points.

7 Draft the firm's promotional campaign for the next six months.

Month	Sales Activity	Advertising	PR	Exhibition	Others
1					
2					
3					
4					
5					
6					

17

Advertising and Merchandising

- **Media advertising is purposeful communication using an identifiable, non-personal, purchased vehicle.**
- **Most media advertising involves a middleman – either the media owner or agency.**
- **Time lags and physical distances stand between the sender of the message and the recipient.**

Introduction and aims

Media advertising takes many forms. It ranges from the glossy and colourful display ads in magazines or on TV to the simple black and white classified ad in a newspaper. Advertising allows the firm to reach many customers with imagery and information. On occasion, through methods such as mail-order, business can be won directly.

This diversity provides many opportunities for the small firm to:

- **Reach prospective or actual customers**
- **Select between different groups**
- **Provide a range of different messages or images**

Here, the different media are introduced, their character explored and practical ways of using them examined.

An abundance of media

Advertising is an industry which has emerged over the last century to meet the many needs of manufacturers and commerce. It has taken many forms, partly because of the variety of needs and partly because of the relative ease of entry into many areas. The advertising business is largely a small firm industry.

Having said this, the more obvious media – TV and national press – are large and mass orientated. Their importance can be exaggerated. Between them they account for less than 50 per cent of total media expenditure. This figure includes a very large amount of classified advertising. Other, less glamorous media, account for the bulk of activity.

The advertising media:

TV	Directories
National newspapers	Radio
Local newspapers	Cinema
Magazines and periodicals	Poster and transport
Trade and technical	Direct mail

A medium exists to suit practically every purpose

The notion of purpose is the key to gaining or obtaining the benefits from advertising. Its most common role is to carry a message to a significant number of prospective or actual customers. The notion of number is important. If these are very small, say single figures, it is unlikely that either sales or benefits will justify the costs in time and money. Reaching large numbers of undifferentiated customers is unlikely to be the aim of the small firm manager. His target market is likely to be restricted and well defined. In all probability this group will have among their common attributes some directly linked to their media use. Engineers might read 'Engineering Today' or hospital administrators 'Hospital Administrator'.

The media used have no value unless the target audience is reached. This is not as straightforward as it may appear. Knowledge of the alternatives, their costs and the groups reached is needed.

The bible of the advertising media planner is *British Rate and Data*

171

(BRAD). This lists virtually all firms and types of advertising with their costs. The most practical way of establishing the magazines, newpapers, etc., used by customers is by asking them. Often the trade publication which comes first to mind – the one you read yourself – is the least useful.

Remember:

Advertise to your customers – not to yourself or your competitors.

In choosing media, the target audience is the starting point. This should be defined very precisely, with their role in the buying act clearly noted and the type of information or image called for defined, in most industrial markets. A number of people are involved in the purchasing decision. They will want their needs met, but probably not in the same way or the same ad. The diversity of needs encourages the latent tendency among managers to include virtually every feature or factor of possible interest in the single advertisement. This is totally counter-productive. Readers are very selective. If it is hard to follow or, at first glance, seems to be written with someone else in mind, it is soon ignored.

Remember:

- You are communicating with individuals, not information processors.
- An advertisement is there to inform, interest, stimulate or prompt action in customers, not as a catalogue of every conceivable feature of the firm or its products.
- Tell customers about the benefits to them.

Cost varies considerably between media. There are a number of dangers in thinking of advertising in terms of the actual price paid. The true cost is the price paid to reach a prospective customer. For this, the idea of Cost Per Thousand (CPT) (or per hundred) is useful. The price of the insertion is related to the number of potential customers reached.

$$CPT = \frac{Cost\ (£)}{Readership \div 1,000}$$

172

Firms choosing apparently low cost media can find themsleves paying far more than their rivals per contact with customers. Absolute costs do matter. There is little point in finding out that the CPT for a national newspaper is half that of a regional one if the cost per insertion is beyond the firm's means.

> *Remember:*
> It is the price of reaching the market in a way which will lead to a result which matters.

Having an impact on the market may mean a number of insertions. Here the firm is faced with the problem of choosing either concentrated and continuous or intermittent advertising. There is no easy way of resolving this problem. The route most likely to pay off involves a recognition that advertising seems to work best when positive trends or developments are accelerating. This means that a seasonal product or a successful new service will benefit most from advertising concentrated when the product or service is on the upswing.

This discussion has concentrated on the structural features of media advertising. The thrust is towards improving productivity and effectiveness. In this, the role of creativity must be recognized. There are no techniques which can be readily applied to stimulate this other than a willingness to be open-minded and customer orientated.

Some simple rules are worth bearing in mind. An advertisement in the media should generally seek to:

1 **Tell a story**
2 **Provide a key idea or visual for the listener/reader/viewer to latch on to**
3 **Grab attention**
4 **Be single-minded**
5 **Register the product or the firm's name**
6 **Have a pay-off for the customer**
7 **Reflect the product or firm's personality**

8 **Avoid jargon and verbiage**

9 **Be part of a campaign**

Merchandising

- Merchandising activity often has the immediate benefit of direct purchase links. It can be used to provide a direct benefit in goods or cash to a client entering a transaction.
- Much of this activity brings customers and sellers together in ways and at a time of the seller's choosing. This can range from a time of year when stocks are high or simply to boost sales for other goals.
- The direct client contact means measurement of performance, control and productivity improvements that are both practical and worthwhile.

Merchandising incorporates a diverse array of techniques and activity areas. Their complexity means that little more than a summary can be given with certain key attributes.

Forms and types of merchandising and non-media activity
These can be divided into consumer and trade, although some can occur in both types.

1 **On pack offers** Anything given away by the producer, physically linked but not the same.
Strength lies in reassuring customers and acting as a reminder to keep company or product name clear.
Weakness is high cost, particularly if given in large numbers to those already buying and loyal. Very unselective.

2 **Free samples** Those not attached to pack or product.
Strength Can introduce the customer at a very low cost to him or her. When the product is significantly superior at a higher price, may be by far the best way of getting trial.
Weakness High cost and risk that product does not meet expectations. Free gifts tend not to create loyalty.

174

3 Free gifts Either totally free or linked to loyalty-building activity, e.g. regular purchase.
Strength Spreads the cost over a number of purchases. This habit of buying can continue after promotion.
Weakness A drain down which large amounts of money can pour. Sometimes very difficult to get off the merry-go-round once customers expect it.

4 Competitions Any activity involving skill by customer or chance.
Strength Generates a real sense of involvement. The limited number of prizes means they can be spectacular, generating a great deal of publicity.
Weakness Massive legal problems and the growing skill of the professional entrant.

5 Exhibitions, trade shows and demonstrations From giants such as the Motor Show to very restricted trade shows.
Strength Large numbers of buyers are brought together under controlled circumstances which the firm can use.
Weakness The quality of the attendance is often in the hands of others. Costs can be considerable. The firm can get into a 'purposeless' habit.

6 Catalogues, leaflets and brochures
Strength Can be precisely targeted with clear guidelines for buyer on how to take action.
Weakness Only as good as their initial design and use.

7 Point-of-sale material
Strength If well designed, can flag the product clearly to customers.
Weakness Growing clutter in retail outlets means reluctance to accept them in better outlets and risk of waste elsewhere.

8 Merchandising back-up Putting own sales force into distributor or retailer.
Strength Adds weight and expertise to middleman's efforts. Can reinforce his loyalty. Generally linked to increased purchases (not at expense of future buying).
Weakness High cost. Risk of negative reaction from other traders.

175

To sum up

There is a tendency to view these types of promotions as separate events to be treated on their own merits. This is fraught with dangers. Objectives for each event should be set, opportunities exploited, but in a wider promotional and marketing context.

The advertising agency: a note

The complexity of the processes described above has led to the emergence of an industry geared to deal with them. A good agency is a tremendous asset. Normally a firm seeking an agency should look for one associated with the Institute of Practitioners in Advertising. This imposes high standards on its members.

The mystique which surrounds media advertising creates many misconceptions about its purposes and operations. Well executed advertising has clear goals and built-in controls. The scope for precision and direction is the cause of the diversity of forms and should not be lost in the plethora of jargon.

Improving the reach, productivity and benefits of media advertising is something any hard-headed small firm manager should strive for. This does mean concentrating on the apparently mundane, not the obviously glamorous. The latter is a servant of the former, not vice versa.

Action Guidelines _____

1 State the goals of the firm's media advertising.

(1) _____

(2) _____

(3) _____

(4) _____

2 Indicate the target audience(s) against which the ads are directed.

(1) _____

(2) _____

(3) _____

3 What features in the advertising meet the:

Awareness _____

_____

Interest _____

_____

Desire _____

_____

Action _____

_____

needs of customers?

4 What is the CPT of media currently used? _____

5 Advertisement, brochure, other literature checklist: Does it:

	Own View	*A Customer's View*
tell a story?	Yes/No	Yes/No
provide a key idea?	Yes/No	Yes/No
grab attention?	Yes/No	Yes/No
act single-mindedly?	Yes/No	Yes/No
register the name?	Yes/No	Yes/No
give a customer pay-off?	Yes/No	Yes/No
reflect the personality?	Yes/No	Yes/No

avoid jargon? | Yes/No | | Yes/No |

play a role in a campaign? | Yes/No | | Yes/No |

6 Identify the most recent non-media promotion embarked on by the firm.

_____

_____

_____

7 Describe the stages in preparation:

(1) Objectives

_____

_____

_____

(2) Pre-promotion contacts (such as invitations to exhibition)

_____

_____

_____

(3) PR pay-offs

_____

_____

_____

(4) Sales/Contacts

_____

_____

_____

(5) Follow-up

_____

_____

_____

(6) What lessons for future initiatives in this area have been learned?

_____

_____

_____

18

Direct Mail

- **Direct mail has been described as the most successful, most precise and potentially most powerful form of advertising.**
- **More effort is probably wasted here than in any other form of advertising.**

Introduction and aims

The key strength of direct mail is that it delivers the firm's message directly into the hands of the prospective buyer. Perhaps surprisingly, the overwhelming majority of them read the message. This is true of both consumer and industrial markets.

The pay-offs from this are primarily a function of:
- **The accuracy of the mailing list**
- **The appropriateness of the offering**
- **The impact of the copy**

The mailing list

The firm's mailing list of customers – current, past, and potential – is a valuable asset. It should be treated as such. The list ought to be carefully examined and refined over time. A well organized mailing will more than pay for itself through business generated throughout the firm's existence. Despite that, firms regularly let their lists degenerate into large jumbles of names. Commercial agencies exist, but often the best source of a good list is the firm's own staff and a willingness to work hard, over time, at getting it right.

The appropriateness of the offering

Even the best prospects will not respond if the timing is wrong or the firm's offering is inappropriate or inadequate.

The impact of the copy

Here are some simple rules:

1 It pays to test the copy and approach with prospects and over time. The test should be in terms of impact and comprehension by customer. You might understand it, but you are not buying it.

2 The coupon is the key to effectiveness. It must be designed to encourage and enable the prospect to respond. It has been estimated that as many as 10 per cent of reply coupons (in industrial markets) are not returned by interested customers because they don't understand how to respond. Generally a coupon is an asset in direct mail.

3 In direct mail every attempt should be made to demonstrate the product, e.g. through free samples, offers of demonstrations or visual representations in copy. The latter must be done well, as poor visuals can kill impact.

4 In general, 'personal' letters and a personal touch should be adopted. Never 'p.p.' a direct mail letter. Try to send to a specific person rather than a title.

5 Although most people read direct mail, they will only dwell for seconds on it. Impact must be immediate and everything must be working for it. Even the envelope can play a part.

6 The copy must be tightly and accurately given. Avoid any errors or mistakes. Generally keep points brief. If possible have a copy strategy which can be developed over time.

7 The opening sentences must grab the reader's attention. Try to think in terms of:

Attention $\longrightarrow$ Interest $\longrightarrow$ Desire $\longrightarrow$ Action

when designing the letter.

8 Although the specific points should be brief, the letter itself can be long, providing the reader's attention is sustained. If the

reader is hooked and believes there is something for him in it, he will persist. Once on the hook, the reader should be led quickly to action (e.g. 'reply by 1st March').

9 If a catalogue or brochure is enclosed it should be closely tied to the letter and the key offers clearly indicated.

10 Normally a higher response rate will be achieved if a premium is offered. This should generally be delivered by the rep in industrial markets. But ensure that the right person is seen.

To sum up

In the direct mail process the manufacturer has a unique opportunity to assess his performance. Response rates, types of reactions and sales should be carefully monitored and the lessons built into successive efforts. The careful, learning firm should eventually end up with a medium of tremendous impact.

Action Guidelines ───────────

1 Does the firm have a customer mailing list?   `Yes/No`
   If YES:
   How is it organized _____

   _____

   Who is responsible for it? _____

   _____

   How comprehensive (of firm's contacts) is it? (Do salesmen, etc.,
   have their own independent lists?) _____

   _____

2 When was the list last 'cleaned' for non-responses or simply new
   information?

   _____

3 Who designs the copy for mailing?

   _____

4 A mailing checklist:

   (1) Has sampling the list shown its rightness?   `Yes/No`

   (2) Has the copy been thoroughly tested?   `Yes/No`

   (3) Is there a response coupon?   `Yes/No`

   (4) Are the product or service attributes brought out   `Yes/No`

   (5) Are all letters addressed personally?   `Yes/No`

   (6) Does opening/introduction have real customer   `Yes/No`
        impact?

   (7) Is it fully proof read?   `Yes/No`

   (8) Is there a customer action hook?   `Yes/No`

   (9) Are support materials linked to letter?   `Yes/No`

   (10) Are there clear cues for a sales follow-up?   `Yes/No`

182

19

Press and Public Relations

- Well organized press and public relations are critical to any small firm.
- Good links with the press can pay enormous dividends.
- These represent very low cost ways of building customer awareness.

Introduction and aims

Two features of successful press and public relations are emphasized here. However the key to success will lie in the willingness of management to overcome their fears and reservations about the media. At the same time the firm needs to recognize that in the firm every month there are news-worthy developments.

The journalist

The man around whom the vast news-gathering network of newspapers, TV, radio, trade and technical papers and magazines is set, is the journalist. Building contacts with him can be a major step in developing a coherent PR policy. Most journalists are more than willing to discuss a small firm's operations, bring out stories and work with management. If it is made clear that certain things are off the record or not yet for publication, this will normally be respected.

A small firm manager should have a line of communication with, or at least be aware of, the industrial journalists on the local newspapers, any relevant nationals, local radio and TV besides writers for the specialist press. The working relationship should be linked with a policy of regular press releases.

Press releases

Two apparently contradictory points should be borne in mind here:

1 Any major newspaper, TV or radio company receives hundreds of press releases every day.
2 It is essential that top management take a very open, liberal view of the newsworthiness of stories in the firm.

Designing a press release is an individual discipline. Any firm with the resources should seriously consider employing a professional PR consultant. For relatively small amounts they will provide invaluable support.

Occasionally the firm will find itself producing its own press releases. The following format has been found to be a relatively useful basis. Note that press releases should always be kept short – preferably less than one page.

Headline If you don't attract the sub-editor's interest you're 'spiked'.

Introductory Paragraph Summarize the entire story in a few key phrases. This may be the only part published.

Manager's Quote The executive in charge or responsible should restate these points but bring out the importance of the development/initiative to the firm.

Detailed Follow-up Paragraphs Two brief paragraphs should fill out the issues noted earlier in ways relevant to the recipient (if a local newspaper, emphasize the local relevance).

Final Comment The executive mentioned above should briefly highlight the importance for the future.

Closing Paragraph This should bring out any human or personal factors in this initiative, jobs or special skills, for instance.

In this a number of details are important.

1 *An editor's note* should be at the bottom of the release. This will give the firm's name, address, telephone number and a reliable contact.

2 Photographs should be included where relevant, but *not* stapled to the letter (unpublishable with holes). On the back of the photograph the firm's name and story headline should be placed. (Don't write or type on photograph.)

To sum up

A firm is part of its community. This wider interest and involvement should be recognized and responded to. A firm with good links in these areas will earn on-going benefits.

Action Guidelines _____

1 Journalist checklist: Name appropriate correspondents.

Local Press	Nationals	Trade & Technical	Radio	TV
_____	_____	_____	_____	_____
_____	_____	_____	_____	_____
_____	_____	_____	_____	_____
_____	_____	_____	_____	_____
_____	_____	_____	_____	_____

2 Identify three 'stories' in the firm today.

(1) _____
_____
_____
_____
_____
_____
_____

(2) _____
_____
_____
_____
_____
_____
_____

(3) _____
_____
_____
_____
_____
_____
_____

20
Selling and Sales Management

- In the marketing operations no-one has a more important role than the salesman.
- Selling involves a combination of skills, knowledge and commitment. Without all three a salesman is not performing his job properly.
- Getting the best out of a sales force calls for concerted and effective management.
- There is much truth in the comment that in Britain the problem isn't selling, it's getting someone to sell to you.

Introduction and aims

The sales force is at the forefront of the marketing effort. Frequently the chief executive spends more time selling than in any other management pursuit. Despite this, salesmen and the selling function are generally undervalued. The salesman's contact with the market is ignored. There is little thought about the selling act. When times are hard it is often this function which is hardest hit by cuts or 'savings'.

Taking the entire small firm community as a group, no single act would earn greater pay-offs than employing more first-class salesmen. This is not likely to take place in the near future, but it is vital that the potential here is recognized. In this chapter some aspects of these 'anti-selling' attitudes will be examined with simple ways of overcoming them identified.

More positively, the different selling tasks will be touched upon.

Readers will have the chance to relate their own actions and those of their staff to the different roles to be fulfilled and jobs to be done. Throughout, the personal nature of the sales force will be returned to regularly. This is important for two reasons:

1 Scope for the individual to express himself ought to be allowed.

2 Management must provide direction and support in a responsive but clear-sighted way.

The successful combination of individual skill and mobilization of resources through management will go a long way to producing real pay-offs.

The salesman

There is a great deal of truth in the notion that a salesman is born, not made. No-one has come up with the perfect model of exactly what a salesman or sales trainer needs to do to produce good results. The value of individuality, creativity, rapport with customers cannot be emphasized enough.

Having said this, in many areas of small firm activity sales standards are abysmal. Too many sales staff have:

- no idea how to handle an enquiry
- dismissive, almost resentful, attitudes to actual or potential customers
- poor product or service knowledge
- no negotiating skills worth mentioning
- sales pitches which owe more to prejudice than planning
- no idea about how to close a sale
- attitudes towards financial issues, notably credit, that should not have been acceptable during the low inflation, high demand 1960s, but can cripple a firm today

An effective salesman, and hence a successful sales force, needs:
- Clear and positive approaches to handling enquiries particularly from new accounts.

- A strategy for following up contacts even when business does not result immediately.
- Supportive attitudes to customers even when they pose problems and try patience. Most small firms are at their best when tackling apparently intractable problems.
- Thorough and current product knowledge including applications and potential developments.
- Studied and effective negotiating strategies.
- A clear and well worked out sales presentation capable of introducing the client to the product, giving an understandable overview while effectively overcoming customer fears or reservation. This should move in a predetermined way to closing the sale.
- Thorough knowledge of financial issues relevant to the sales activity. This should include sufficient expertise to adapt to special or difficult circumstances.

Many analysts of sales/customer relationships have noted that more customers are turned off than are won – this takes into account the disinterested customer.

Improved sales force productivity is achievable and desirable for both parties.

The good salesman is an asset of enormous value; the poor one a total liability.

Warning signs

A manager should regularly search out the warning signs for poor sales development.

Warning signs include:
- **Little boxes**
- **Favourite faces**
- **Hard travelling**
- **Bookworms**

Little boxes This is a favoured strategy in retail selling. The salesman builds a wall around himself which the customer must penetrate to attract his attention and interest. The best examples probably lie in the motor trade where salesmen congregate in glass cubicles while prospects come in, look at the cars and go out. The inactivity is justified on the spurious grounds that 'they weren't serious anyway – or they'd have come to me'. This is a comment that can go both ways. Neither is the salesman.

In other areas of retail selling, the stocklist, the cleaning rag, even the sales display can usefully protect the salesman or woman from the customer.

In manufacturing or services equally, subtle strategies have emerged with the telephone and personal secretary being impenetrable, particularly in combination. Sales force productivity can be massively improved by breaking down these walls and simply letting the customer through to buy. At regular intervals the concerned manager should objectively check on the responsiveness and outwardness of his staff, preferably incognito or through someone he can trust.

Favourite faces In selling, like any other area of activity, it is easiest to follow the route of least resistance. Most salesmen have favoured groups of customers. These are often fairly small accounts but carefully nurtured. These may be good for a pleasant discussion, even willing to come up with very small orders to 'justify' the visit.

Often these calls merit neither the time nor the back-up which tends to grow as links are built. Relationships are often cemented in ways totally disfunctional to the company – below minimum order size, delayed payment, etc.

The pattern of visiting should be closely controlled with returns monitored. This should combine prospecting, customer service and order collection with new, established and lost accounts. The balance here will need to be judged carefully in conjunction with the sales person.

The salesman should be required to indicate into which category each visit falls. Justifying the pattern which emerges can become part of a regular performance review.

Figure 29 *Sales activity matrix*

	Order collection	Client service	Prospecting
Established accounts			
Lost accounts			
New business leads			

Hard travelling   This is probably the commonest problem of all in manufacturing and services. The salesman sees himself being judged in terms of mileage, not revenue. The more distant the client, the greater his potential.

Under most circumstances the salesman can only work at his best when he is in front of a customer.

The challenge:
- Maximize Eye Contact Time.

There are limits on this. Order processing has to take place. Trouble-shooting is needed. Batteries have to be recharged. Despite this, devices to increase Eye Contact Time should be constantly sought.

One way of doing this may seem to go against the notion. Telephone selling is well worth investigating. It does involve special skills but, properly done, can dramatically increase contact rates particularly with those distant clients so beloved of the hard travelling man.

Bookworms   These are another form of protection from the customer. The salesman simply spends less and less time on the road. The strategies for doing this are various, but include:

> The orders have piled up and I've got to get them right.
>
> I've been doing some research that I'm sure will pay off.
>
> I'd like to take a more marketing approach.

Sometimes these express a situation which is developing – all too often they do not. The way of overcoming it is the same as that for the hard travelling man.

Sales force tasks and skills

Having recognized the behavioural warning signs, it is necessary to recognize the seven basic tasks. In part or in whole, in different combinations, they describe the job to be done:

1 **Product delivery**
2 **Inside order taking**
3 **Outside order taking**
4 **Goodwill building**
5 **Technical and engineering representation**
6 **Creative selling of tangibles**
7 **Creative selling of intangibles**

Performing these tasks effectively calls for a number of related skills:
- **Product knowledge**
- **Market knowledge**
- **Prospecting**
- **Sales pitching or presenting**
- **Closing or completing sale**
- **Follow-up**

The effective salesman needs *all* these to perform *any* of the tasks identified earlier.

To sum up

In many small firms the chief executive is the only or leading salesman. If he is to be effective, he will need to meet the exacting standards of *the most difficult job in marketing.* It demands resources and a professionalism which too many small firms skimp, to their cost.

Action Guidelines

1 Check for:

Little Boxes _____

_____

_____

_____

_____

_____

Favourite Faces _____

_____

_____

_____

_____

_____

Hard Travelling _____

_____

_____

_____

_____

Bookworm _____

_____

_____

_____

_____

Other Anti-Customer Devices _____

_____

_____

_____

_____

_____

2 The Sales Activity Matrix (to be completed for each salesman, including self):

	Order collection	Client service	Prospecting
Established accounts			
Lost accounts			
New business leads			

3 Eye Contact Time Audit:

Salesman	Current %	Target %

4 Review of areas/activities where telephone selling has a role:

_____

_____

_____

_____

_____

_____

_____

5 Checklist for last test of:

	Salesman A	Salesman B	Salesman C
(1) Product knowledge			
(2) Market knowledge			
(3) Prospecting activities			
(4) Sales pitch aptness			
(5) Closure strategies			
(6) Follow-ups			

21
Recruitment, Selection, Management, Motivation and Control of Salesmen

- **A sales force is as good as its sales management.**
- **All the tasks identifed in the chapter title have a role and significance.**

Introduction and aims

The importance and demands of managing a sales force are poorly reflected in the skill, time and effort used in studying, reflecting upon and arriving at solutions to the problems involved in building and maintaining quality. Two beliefs dominate:

> If you recruit the right man, it will work out all right.
>
> The commission system will motivate and control endeavours.

This is a poor picture of reality. Salesmen spend far too much time outside the firm, operate in too many complex and demanding areas for such simplistic notions to work.

In this section the diverse and challenging tasks involved in effective sales management are discussed. The notion that salesmen must be self-motivated is rejected. Personal drive must exist but can be too easily misdirected or eradicated by poor management.

Part of the management process

In many ways sales force management is the same as any other aspect of company management. The skills in interpersonal communication, sensitivity and responsiveness must combine with a view of the direction in which the firm is going and the contribution this part of its operation is making. A special problem facing the sales manager lies in the external nature of the selling job. Most staff will spend the bulk of their time outside the firm. This can lead to an unhealthy degree of identification with the customer, not the firm. The process of management motivation and control needs to be particularly directed at managing this peculiar *boundary definition problem.*

A footwear company in the East Midlands discovered this problem early in its life. It had been established by two brothers. During its early years most jobs had been shared but one had spent much of his time selling. As the firm grew, he had to stay in the office more and more. First one, then another new salesman was appointed. However both brothers were disappointed in their performance. Sales growth was slow, orders were often unprofitable and the salesmen seemed 'to spend more time representing customer interests to us, than selling'. The problem was that no attempt had been made to fully integrate the new salesmen into day to day operations. They spent 80 to 90 per cent of their time with customers. Perhaps inevitably, they ended up identifying with them. The *boundaries* of their loyalties had been *defined* to include customers but exclude their employer.

Recruitment and selection

Skills in these areas will determine the material with which the manager will be working.

They call for:
- a clear job description.
- an extensive search using contacts as well as more formal methods such as advertising.

- thorough evaluation of applications and references. This should never be an individual job. Others should be involved. If the firm is too small, go outside for advice and help.
- a carefully designed screening system.
- thorough interviews, probably involving more than one meeting with all short-listed candidates, at least one being in an informal setting.
- clear definition of terms and conditions with *no* unfulfillable promises.
- a sensible and planned induction programme, including training.
- an agreed review period.

Management, motivation and control

For most salesmen, an informal management style, providing it is both directive and decisive, is effective. This assumes the other more general aspects of management are under control.

Motivation is generally poorly understood in small firms. In achieving specific results, financial inducements are remarkably ineffective.

The most important are:
- **A sense of achievement** for jobs well done
- **Recognition**
- **Control** over tasks and clear areas of **responsibility**
- **Opportunities** for personal advancement
- **Appreciation of the role** they play and the value of their work to the firm

Small firms are particularly well placed to provide these motivators. By organizing their approach they can increase substantially their benefits at a low cost.

Control is more dependent on financial factors and directions. A well planned commission system can provide a framework for effective management control. It is worth recognizing that a balance between basic salary and commission should exist which combines security with efficiency and inducements with control.

Targets can play a vital part. When they are arrived at in an open, discussed way – *NOT* imposed arbitrarily – they almost always improve returns. Of particular interest to top management involved in selling, self-imposed targets are by far the most effective.

To sum up

Sales management is a vital task demanding close scrutiny and careful organization. Effectiveness in the blend of activities described above will determine the long-term efficiency of the marketing effort.

22
Getting the Best from Middlemen

- **Middlemen are all those outside the firm involved in the movement of goods or services from producer to consumer.**
- **They constitute the networks of intermediaries linking this process together.**
- **These intermediaries, retail and wholesale, face their own special market conditions with resulting demands.**

Introduction and aims

Relatively few companies deal directly with their end customers. The overwhelming majority deal through some intermediary, whether wholesaler, retailer, mail-order house or some specialized form such as a timber merchant or a steel stockholder. These middlemen play a vital part in breaking down the volumes produced by the manufacturer into smaller quantities which can be bought by the consumer. They give the producer access to markets which he never otherwise could reach. Despite their importance to them, many small firms do not take a structured or planned approach to their intermediaries and channels of distribution. Accounts are opened, relationships developed, with little purpose other than winning extra business in the short term.

The nature of these relationships makes this a dangerous policy. The links established are long-term. In some markets, particularly overseas, they are legally enforceable.

A Liverpool based firm of electrical contractors found this out, to their cost, in the Gulf states. The distributor they had recruited made little or no attempt to promote their goods. When they attempted to withdraw their agency, however, he successfully sued for massive costs.

A golf club manufacturer found a similar pattern in Sweden. Their agent had totally misled them for a number of years. He had charged very high prices while paying them very little. Their decision to cut off links with him cost them the distribution network they had financed him to develop. The dealerships established with the golf professionals were with the agent not the manufacturer.

The company using a particular intermediary often cannot extract itself easily if difficulties arise or warning signs appear.

The clothing industry over the last ten years epitomizes the problems and risks of this. The fate of many small manufacturers

Figure 30   *Trading patterns*

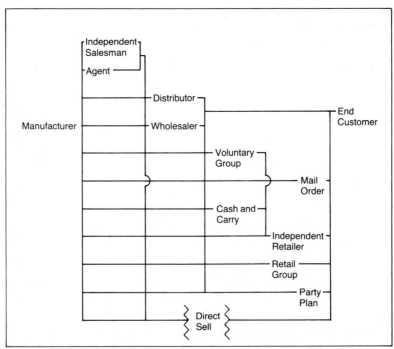

is totally outside their control. They depend entirely on the success or failure of certain retailers or wholesalers. In the clothing industry the price of this has been paid when major accounts have contracted or firms collapsed.

The aim of this unit is to look at these relationships. The extent to which firms can make real choices will be examined. Intermediary and channel policies are part of the marketing mix. This means that the firm has a control over its destiny that might not be clear at a particular moment in time.

Alternatives and opportunities

A manufacturer or trader has alternatives open to him as he seeks to reach his end customer. These operate at different levels; some he will deal with directly, others through another intermediary; some of his middlemen will not deal directly with the end user themselves. This is shown in Figure 30.

This figure describes just some of the forms of intermediary that exist to get goods from producer to end customer.

In designing the network of intermediaries, the firm has four basic options:

- *Intensive distribution;* seek every possible outlet for the firm's product.
- *Selective distribution;* outlets are chosen but within a fairly broad category, pharmacists for instance.
- *Exclusive distribution;* the intermediary is chosen very carefully and then given exclusive rights to an area of product line.
- *Vertical integration;* the producer can become directly involved in selling.

This last alternative probably needs some explanation, particularly in the context of small firms. It means that the producer or middleman integrates all the stages in the process from producer to consumer under his ownership.

The Burton Group proudly boasted that it handled every stage 'from sheep to shop'.

Over the last decade, Church's, the shoe manufacturers, have steadily built up their own footwear retailing network. This provides them with the high quality outlets needed to sell their shoes successfully.

A Craft Guild in the West of England purchased a shop in Bristol and later one in London to give them access to a large market.

The most obvious forms of vertical integration in smaller companies lie in the activities of those craftsmen who buy their own retail shop or companies who become involved in party plan operations, like clothing manufacturers.

The essential feature of these alternatives is that the decisions involve choices. The company is controlling its own destiny. Without choice, the company's destiny will lie in the hands of others.

The established middleman

Relatively few firms are in the business of setting up a wholly new intermediary system. Most have established trading relationships which they are seeking to make the best of, often in difficult circumstances. Earlier, some observations on this were made. Particular emphasis was given to the need to understand one's customer almost as fully as one understands oneself. Planning a network means thinking it through to its conclusion, examining the nature, form and future of the business prospects of the intermediary in question. Without that, the firm is in no position to argue or contrast its experience with that of the trader.

Wholesale and retail marketing

The approach of many writers and commentators to marketing often seems to imply that wholesalers and retailers exist merely to serve the needs of the manufacturing sector. Their marketing problems are ignored in the curious belief that:

> **❝** a wholesaler or retailer is involved in a safe, secure or easy business, or retail marketing merely involves fitting in with the plans of manufacturers. **❞**

Nothing can be further from the truth. Most retail markets are highly competitive, with success going to those with a clear vision of their *own* market. Their offering, its strengths, weaknesses and opportunities, has to be thought through.

Intermediaries need to bring the same type of marketing commitment to their operations, particularly in drawing together their different offerings of location, range of goods, method of display and selling activity. Smaller retailers, wholesalers and other intermediaries have been under strong competitive pressure recently. The increased sophistication of their larger rivals, allied to discriminatory policies by some larger manufacturers, has placed them in a difficult position. Effective marketing provides the only coherent way of overcoming these twin problems.

This effectivess will turn upon the construction of:
- **A clear image of the customer group catered for**
- **A precise picture of the total offering the company is making**
- **An effective balance between service, hours of opening and internal requirements**

Retailers, wholesalers and other intermediaries will need to bear in mind the marketing mix issues discussed in the earlier sections of this book.

The reluctance of some small traders and intermediaries to think long and hard about their customers puts them at a disadvantage. This comes in part from a sense that this should have been done already for them by the manufacturer. Although there is some overlap of interest, the small retailer, wholesaler and other intermediary will, perhaps inevitably, stand or fall on his own devices.

Supplier push and customer pull

A successful middleman needs to balance pressures from suppliers with demands from customers in a way which reinforces his competitiveness. The pattern of 'push' and 'pull' provides a coherent structure for this.

The speed of movement of goods through the distribution system will turn on how well the manufacturer balances:

- **His trade push:** the pressure to stock, display and promote the item.
- **His customer pull:** the positive action by other middlemen or end users seeking out the item or range.

Most middlemen will not carry a line which their customers do not buy, regardless of the incentives or discount. An emerging form of this is in developing markets where specification of an item for inclusion in a package involving a vast range of goods and services is increasingly important.

To sum up

The complexity of the modern industrial society will tend to push the manufacturer further and further away from the end user of his product. Channels of distribution of increasing complexity will emerge to fill the gap. However, unless the small manufacturer determines to control this, he will soon find himself as much a slave to the trader as the employee is a wage slave to his boss.

Action Guidelines _____

1 List actions geared to:
   Trade Push   Customer Pull

   _____   _____
   _____   _____
   _____   _____
   _____   _____
   _____   _____

2 Detail measures adopted to keep intermediaries informed of actions
   to generate customer pull.

   _____
   _____
   _____
   _____
   _____
   _____
   _____
   _____
   _____

3 What actions are taken to ensure balance?

   _____
   _____
   _____
   _____
   _____
   _____
   _____
   _____
   _____

23
Physical Distribution Management

- This has been described as 'the Economy's dark continent'. It reflects a situation in which massive costs are incurred but are seldom easily attributed to particular areas.
- The history of neglect means that initiatives here offer among the most promising opportunities for major reductions in costs and improvements in profits. These can have tangible short-term benefits besides making a long-term contribution to business development.
- Integration of the activities involved is vital if real success is to be achieved.

The scope of physical distribution

The rapid increase in inflation in the late 1970s caused many firms to look long and hard at their costs.

Among these was a furniture manufacturer based in the Midlands. The owner decided to have a thorough overhaul of his costs particularly in terms of the reasons for their existence, the benefits earned by them and the frequency with which they were reviewed. He was particularly alarmed at the casual approach adopted to those broadly defined as 'distribution costs'. Looking through the process by which materials bought in were coverted to saleable products, he found:

206

1 Very high stocks of raw materials. Some of these had deteriorated because of the time in stock. A number of special materials were held for lines or customer requirements that seldom occurred.

2 Large stocks of finished or semi-finished products often exceeding likely demand. The cost of retaining these was seldom seriously reviewed.

3 A fleet of vehicles geared to a level of service and speed of delivery that far exceeded customer requirements 'but was very useful when schedules fell behind'.

4 Delays in invoicing that doubled, even trebled the effective credit period.

5 Recurrent errors in delivery schedules which meant that over 30 per cent of these were incomplete or inaccurate.

The final assessment was that together these added 8 per cent to his costs with no commercial benefit.

Physical distribution incorporates all those activities designed to move the goods or services produced by the firm, in the right quantities, in an acceptable form, from the point of origin to the point of consumption. As an area of activity it incorporates virtually 30 per cent of all economic activity – shipping, freighting, packaging, storing, protecting, processing and handling. This means, for a particular firm, that about a quarter of its costs are likely to be tied up this way. Often there is an unjustified sense of powerlessness about these costs because they are highly fragmented or difficult to separate from other activities. The essential feature of the marketing approach to physical distribution is the recognition that these areas are not solely *cost centres*, but are *opportunity areas*.

Problems and opportunities

No area of marketing activity more clearly illustrates the scope for small firms to gain differential advantage over larger rivals than physical distribution. This turns on the intimate link between *the provision* of the facilities for physical distribution:

Transport
Materials handling
Packaging
Warehousing
Inventory

Location
Order and item processing
Back-up

and *the benefit* sought through the provision of **service**.

The small firm manager's combination of commitment to the latter and flexibility with the former provides real advantages.

These are incorporated in an approach in fairly regular use today:

- **The total cost approach to distribution**

This plays down the separateness of the facilities described above – divisions sometimes required by the bureaucratic nature of large firms. The importance of managing the pay-offs and transfer of costs is highlighted. All too often in large firms, warehouses, purchasing, traffic and other managers respond to pressure to cut costs in ways which have a direct effect on the other related areas. The stores manager's decision to run down stocks will make his budgets look good. However, it might mean purchasing in smaller, less economical quantities. The traffic manager could end up with multiple deliveries to meet orders. The result is overall increases in cost with reduced services.

> This occurred with an electrical goods retailer in London. A company-wide cost cutting exercise led the manager of the parts department to slash his stocks. This meant that service engineers were carrying a much smaller range of parts on their vehicles. The result was that the frequency with which repairs were completed on the first visit dropped from 65 per cent to 40 per cent. The number of customer complaints about delays increased so much that the firm took on two new girls to process these. The 5 per cent saving for the stores manager produced major increases in costs elsewhere.

A marketing orientated manager should have his finger on the pulse of all these activities. His in-depth knowledge, plus awareness of their interactions, gives him both the information and authority to balance these pay-offs, costs and efforts to reduce costs while improving services. His aim here will be to wed action to clear company goals and purposes.

To sum up

Modern technologies are already transforming this area. The next decade will see a revolution of new communication systems geared to process information at a phenomenal pace and wedded to new delivery and ordering systems. Companies with poor distribution systems will struggle to compete with firms with a high level of appreciation of opportunities in this area.

24

Exports and International Marketing

- Britain is, and has been for many years, one of the world's great exporting nations.
- This turns largely on the skill and expertise of management involved in international trade.
- Developing business overseas calls for matching established marketing skills with specific disciplines in exporting.

Introduction and aims

Recently there has been growing recognition of the vital role that small firms can play in Britain's economy. Flexibility, adaptability, decisiveness and innovativeness are assets in any attempt to win business overseas.

This was brought out very clearly in the Barclays Bank report 'Export Development in France, Germany and the United Kingdom' (1978). Here it came out very clearly that the ability to adapt to customer needs and respond creatively to their requirements is a major asset to the exporter:

 It has always been a marked characteristic of progressive and successful companies engaged in international trade to keep the market buoyant by a policy of constant product improvement and the development of new designs. *Barclays Bank Report*

In this process of improvement and adaptation to buyer needs, freedom of action, management discretion and a high level of practical, technical knowledge are powerful aids. Here the owner or senior manager of the small to medium sized firm has many advantages over his competitor in the larger firm.

Cost is usually seen as the main barrier to export development by smaller firms. Many reports and numerous examples of managerial ingenuity show the exports that can be won through recognizing that developments to meet market needs do not necessarily involve the high costs sometimes associated with advanced technology.

At home smaller firms base their efficiency on close links with actual or prospective buyers, access to an extensive information 'grapevine' and detailed industry knowledge. A similar level of awareness overseas is needed to exploit export potential to the full.

This calls for:
- **Effectively mobilizing the firm's resources**
- **Identifying the key market opportunities**
- **Using the array of support services and agencies**
- **Giving overseas markets an appropriate level of marketing support and service**
- **Careful planning**
- **Building a strong export organization**

This in turn means going through a number of carefully thought out steps.

The first step

The first question the would-be exporter need ask is: 'Am I ready to export?'

The answer to this question lies in a number of factors, some outside of his control. Before examining this he should check whether or not he is already exporting. If he is, the question might be better phrased 'Am I getting the best out of my current export links?'

Unless the firm is already effectively mobilizing its resources or willing to do so, the answer to both will be **no**.

Resources and skills

The key to successful export marketing for the smaller firm normally lies in matching its resources and skills with the opportunities that exist in foreign markets. Absolute lack of resources is seldom the true problem. Appreciating the true, key resources and directing these effectively is essential. Most firms lack the resources to introduce product or design changes to meet the special needs of export customers during the initial period of export market development. As confidence grows and links with these new markets develop, design and development changes to suit their new customers' needs will grow in importance, but not yet! During the initial development period it is the use of existing resources which provides the key to success.

The following are critical:

- **Attitude:** Is exporting a real company priority?
- **Awareness:** Is there a basic knowledge to capitalize on?
- **Previous experience:** Are existing links being used properly?
- **Product characteristics and mix:** Can the firm adapt?
- **Service and delivery history:** If problems occurred before, can they be overcome?
- **Financial situation:** Do the resources exist to start seriously?
- **Corporate activity:** What skills can be exploited?

Small firms can gain enormous benefits from the short lines of communication, easy access to key staff and overall cohesion that is typical of this type of firm. In particular, the top manager is generally in a position to lead the firm more clearly and quickly in the direction he wishes to go. He will normally have a greater detailed understanding of the full range of the firm's capabilities than the chief executive of the large concern. People, attitudes, knowledge, expertise, product offerings, finance and accumulated technical skills can be mobilized to win exports. His determination to succeed, often despite setbacks, will set the standards for the rest of the firm. The desire to succeed is not sufficient, unless it is backed by top management action.

Concentration for profits

Most firms find that concentration of effort plays a major role in realizing export potential.

❛ Some of the most successful companies tend to concentrate (as a matter of conscious policy) on a few products or a few markets. They can thus make a bigger impact even when the resources they can employ in some sectors are modest. **❜** *The Betro Report 1977*

Trying to export the company's entire range means:

1 **Dissipating efforts**
2 **Failure to distinguish real export product prospects from mainstay home products**
3 **Confusion about the target markets**
4 **Difficulties in negotiations with end users or intermediaries over the precise nature of the firm's offerings**
5 **Lack of precision in the sales and marketing effort**
6 **Extra work in building up a full picture of tariffs, customs dues and regulations**

Success comes from maximum effort behind the firm's greatest assets that is those with real potential overseas.

This notion of concentration is at least *as* important in discussing markets. The Betro report highlighted the value of concentration on key markets. Too often firms invest a great deal of effort into a large number of markets with the overwhelming bulk of business and profits coming from a small number – the classic 80:20 rule.

Selecting the market

At the centre of successful exporting is the selection of those markets in which the firm's output is:

- Likely to be demanded
- Can be serviced
- Earns a good return for the producer

A company based in Filey discovered this in a particularly vivid way. Traditionally it had exported to Cyprus and Malta. Political changes during the 1970s reduced the value of this business. The Managing Director decided to go on a selling trip to Holland and Belgium. The nature of their lines meant that sales trips to the West Country and Scotland were fairly common but this was the first overseas one to mainland Europe. Setting off on Wednesday, he went first to the BOTB offices in Leeds, then to Hull where he took the ferry to the Hook of Holland. He arrived early Thursday. The next days were spent visiting potential customers. He even managed a visit to a Trade Fair in Antwerp. Although he was surprised by the ease of establishing links, his biggest shock was from a simple fact. During his travels he 'clocked-up' 485 miles – far less than the distance he would travel to sell in either the West Country or Scotland.

The best market will be that best suited to the resources of the firm. The biggest market for giftware may be the USA, but a company based near Harwich is more likely to earn real profits by concentrating on the Benelux markets it can reach quickly, easily and frequently.

A Midlands plastics company found that a Dutch firm they had been supplying with a standard item for five years at average annual sales of £20,000 per annum, was the largest distributor of this type of product in Holland and Belgium. Careful examination of this firm's catalogue showed that the firm could produce 20 of its lines, not just the one currently supplied. After two years' serious effort it was supplying 14 lines with an annual sale of £360,000.

Figure 31 *A firm's network of possible points of contact with export markets*

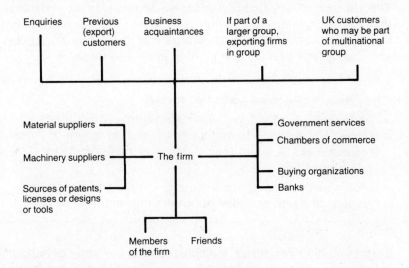

A review of the firm's network of contacts can play a major part in highlighting key opportunities.

The potential exporter should steadily work his way through this network. Even very small firms have access to an enormous range of overseas contacts, volumes of information, massive help and even substantial funds. It can be used to win business.

The confusion between markets and countries should be avoided. A market is the area in which business can be won. It might be a specific customer-industry or group of customers in a country. It might cross national boundaries, as in the case of the quality car producers. The firm looking to concentrate its resources can earn as much from focusing on a key group such as this, as on a specific geographical area. Whichever route is adopted, UK businessmen are fortunate in having access to a wide array of support services.

Support agencies

The UK exporter probably has access to more direct assistance than exporters in any other country. However, many firms (notably the smaller concerns) remain unaware of the range of support services or face problems in gaining access to them.

The problem of access takes two forms:

- An inability to structure enquiries in forms which these bodies can respond to and a corresponding failure of these organizations to adapt their patterns of response to meet fully small firms' needs.
- Problems of mismatch, particularly in time scales and the amount of detail provided about the firm and its enquiries.

Even in highly specialized, individual cases, the array of support facilities is so wide that many of their needs can be met. Among the major support agencies are: The British Overseas Trade Board, Banks, Trade Associations, Chambers of Commerce, Industry Training Boards and Industry Research Associations. All are becoming more aware of the need to tailor services to special needs of smaller firms. Special BOTB services for small firms such as the 'Market Entry Guarantee Scheme' now exist. Help can range from the collection of information to direct financial support for Export Market Research.

Despite the array of services, most managers of small concerns are fully aware that the onus for success lies with them, not with these outside agencies, helpful as they may be.

Building up the market

In achieving success in exports, a sustained marketing effort to reach the key markets is vital. A simple comparison between the way the firm operates at home and its export operations can highlight many important issues.

One footwear manufacturer drew up a simple model of how accounts were opened in Britain compared with his hitherto abortive efforts at exporting. He found that his tendency to conduct all contracts by letter, his lack of personal follow-up, notably to quotations, and his dependence on outsiders such as agents was in stark contrast to his personal, sustained, active follow-up of prospects on the home market. As soon as he moved closer to the approach he used at home, orders started being won.

The right form of overseas representation is critical to any small firm. There has been a common belief that the 'hungry' agent was a universal panacea. Once appointed, he would provide a ready source of business, requiring only the occasional meeting at an exhibition or fair to keep sales up. More firms are realizing that recruitment, selection, management, motivation and control of an agent in West Germany is as important as it is for the firm's salesman in West Hartlepool.

An East Anglian boat builder took a highly systematic approach to finding the right dealers. He started by drawing up a detailed job description including a profile of the type of firm sought.

This was followed up by an exhaustive search of his contacts in complementary areas, like other non-competitive boat builders, searching through the literature of others to spot good agents, advertising in magazines and using the agency finding services of the BOTB and his bank.

The list that was built up was then pruned through checking references and other means. This produced a short-list.

He then spent four days visiting the firms on his list. Prior to this he found out as much as possible about the market. This data was checked by visits to the commercial attachés and other contacts in the market. Following this process he was well able to make a considered choice.

This growing consciousness that effectively working in a market, even through agents, involves real investment in time, money and other resources has encouraged some smaller firms to explore the scope for direct representation. Although higher costs may be involved under certain circumstances, improved performance, particularly in industrial markets and specifically technical or process industries, can lead to significantly better returns.

Organization and planning

The construction of a more professional export initiative is needed as competition hots up. A system geared to ensure that orders gained overseas are not lost in the factory is essential. At the same time, export marketing planning has a role to play in ensuring that a sustained and improving export performance emerges.

In small firms an informal organization probably pays the best dividends. It should bring together the various functions of production, sales, design and research and development. Often most of these will be encapsulated in one man – the owner. Even here, others should be involved, if only to provide the on-going encouragement and reassurance needed when the inevitable barriers and problems occur.

Export planning poses one of the most serious challenges to the entrepreneur. Often the business has been built far more on flexibility and speed than on a plan. Despite this, the distances, the newness of situations and the costs mean that some form of planning is called for. The simple but effective planning approach described earlier, but adapted for exports, can be effectively used within the resources of the small firm.

To sum up

British industry – large, medium and small – has a real responsibility for resolving our longer term industrial problems. The small firm sector is probably the area most capable of responding quickly to the situation. There are many signs for hope. However, these indications need to be effectively capitalized upon by others in smaller concerns and, ultimately, the rest of British industry. It ought to be recognized that the skills which have kept Britain as one of the world's most successful trading nations still encompass those capable of reversing the negative trends.

Export marketing checklist:
to assist in the go/no go decision

The primary aim of the checklist is to identify, through the questions, the key areas of company capability. At the same time, it highlights the aspects of the firm's activities and resources which require development to realize fully export opportunities.

Attitude

1 Are the chief executive and other senior staff willing to spend a significant proportion of their time on exporting?

YES/NO (other comments) _____

_____

_____

_____

_____ (10)

2 Is the firm willing and able to devote major resources to exporting?

YES/NO (other comments) _____

_____

_____

_____

_____ (5)

Awareness

3 Is there a range of experience of foreign travel in the firm?

YES/NO (details) _____

_____

_____

_____ (1)

4 Do any members of the firm have extensive experience of other countries?

YES/NO (details) _____

_____

_____

_____

_____

_____ (

5 Do any members of the firm speak any foreign languages well?

YES/NO (details) _____

_____

_____

_____

_____ (

6 Do any members of the firm's staff have experience of business dealings abroad?

YES/NO (details) _____

_____

_____

_____

_____ (

Previous experience

7 Have any members of the firm's management any experience of export selling?

YES/NO (details) _____

_____

_____

_____ (

8 Has the firm exported before?
YES/NO (details) _____

_____
_____
_____
_____ (3)

9 Did the firm search out the order(s)?
YES/NO (describe how the order(s) came)

_____
_____

_____
_____ (2)

10 Has the company had follow-up orders from the same source?
YES/NO (details) _____

_____
_____
_____ (5)

11 Has the firm had follow-up orders from related sources?
YES/NO (details) _____

_____
_____
_____ (2)

12 Is the firm now in a position to better exploit any opportunities
that occur?
YES/NO _____

_____
_____
_____
_____ (3)

Product

13 Can you identify certain products or capabilities from your array of products and capabilities with real export potential?

YES/NO (list) _____

_____

_____

_____

_____ (2

14 Does your product(s)* have a major advantage over:
   (a) UK competitors?
   (b) Foreign competitors?

YES/NO (specify) _____

(a) _____

_____ (2

(b) _____

_____

_____ (2

15 Does your product technology provide the flexibility in process and form often required in foreign markets?

YES/NO (describe) _____

_____

_____

_____

_____ (3

16 Does your product design and development require a close working relationship with customers?

YES/NO _____

_____

_____

_____

_____ (2

* From this point the term product is used to describe a single specific product, an array of products or a capability to manufacture to order or specification.

222

17 Are you in a position to provide this service to export customers?

YES/NO _____

_____

_____

_____ (5)

18 Is your record of delivery times good?

Over 80 per cent arrive on or before promised delivery date | Yes/No | (8)

Over 60 per cent arrive on or before promised delivery date | Yes/No | (4)

Over 40 per cent arrive on or before promised delivery date | Yes/No | (2)

19 Do you have the capacity to meet major export orders?

YES/NO (specify) _____

_____

_____

_____ (5)

Finance

20 Does your chief financial adviser believe that you can happily enter export markets?

YES/NO _____

_____

_____ (3)

21 Are you willing to set aside funds to develop export markets if opportunities arise?

YES/NO _____

_____

_____

_____ (10)

Corporate activity

22 Does your firm have a history of innovation in product and design?

YES/NO (specify) _____

_____

_____

_____ (3)

23 Do you have experience of dealing through intermediaries?

YES/NO _____

_____

_____

24 Are you familiar with selling processes involving extensive documentation?

YES/NO _____

_____

_____

_____ (2)

25 Are you familiar with the use of external agencies – government, market research?

YES/NO (specify) _____

_____

_____

_____ (3)

Total

The figures in brackets at the end of each question provide a weighting for each factor. The totals arrived at provide some *guidelines* to indicate whether the firm is geared to profitable exporting. These are not absolute indicators and the efficient choice of product market and intermediary can lead to profitable exports although the scores are low. However, a score below *35* should cast doubts over entering exporting without a very serious re-examination of the firm's resources.

Sources of Market Information

It is very difficult to provide a wholly comprehensive list of all the sources of market information available in Britain today. The task becomes even more difficult if the attempt to summarize includes Europe and the rest of the world. Attempts have been made and are still being made to do this. Among the more valuable sources are:

E. Tupper and G. Wills, *Sources of UK Marketing Information*, Ernest Benn, 24 New Street Square, London EC4. However, its in-depth coverage of Government statistics has since been superseded to a considerable extent by *Guide to Official Statistics*, HMSO, London Region, Atlantic House, Holborn Viaduct, London EC1.

More affordable is:
Christine Hull, *Principal Sources of Marketing Information*, Times Information and Market Intelligence Unit, New Printing House Square, Gray's Inn Road, London WC1.

Also useful for detailed industry information are:
UK Market Guide, IMAC Research, Esher, Surrey.
The A–Z of UK Marketing Information, Euromonitor Ltd, 18 Doughty Street, London WC1.
MNG Marketing Manual, Mirror Group of Newspapers.
Statistical Analyses of British Industry, Market Location Ltd, 17 Waterloo Place, Warwick Street, Royal Leamington Spa, Warwickshire CV32 5LA.

All these sources provide overviews of the British market while providing the opportunity to gather specific information on specific industries. Each provides the foundation for invaluable data.

No examination of the sources of statistics for industry is complete without reference to:
The Annual Abstract of Statistics, HMSO. This summarizes the key statistics collected by the Central Statistical Office.

International data is more variable in quality while posing special problems of collation and comparison. One of the most valuable sources of data here is:

The International Directory of Published Market Research, British Overseas Trade Board in conjunction with Arlington Management Publications Ltd, Jermyn Street, London SW1.

A more detailed – and more expensive! – listing of market research data is: *Findex*, ICC Information Group, City Road, London EC1.

For those seeking more specific information and statistics:

Subjects Indexed to Sources of Comparative International Statistics, CBD Research, High Street, Beckenham, Kent.

International Marketing Data and Statistics, Euromonitor Publications Ltd, 18 Doughty Street, London WC1.

Concise Guide to International Markets, International Advertising Association in conjunction with Leslie Stinton and Partners, London Road, Kingston-on-Thames, Surrey.

Besides these market based sources, the leading international agencies publish major statistical reviews on a regular basis. Particularly:

United Nations:
Directory of International Statistics
Demographic Yearbook
Yearbook of Industrial Statistics
Statistical Yearbook
Yearbook of National Accounts Statistics

International Monetary Fund:
Balance of Payments Yearbook
Directions of World Trade

Organization of Economic Co-operation and Development:
Economic Outlook
International Tourism and Tourist Policies

These sources provide information on a world-wide basis. However, most firms will be particularly interested in information on particular regions or countries.

European information sources

Anyone interested in highly specialized information on a specific European market should recognize that most leading industrial countries have reached a roughly similar level of sophistication in data gathering and dissemination. All major European countries publish national market data through the equivalent of the Central Statistical Office or private marketing or market research agencies. Europe-wide data is published by a number of organizations:

European Marketing and Statistics, Euromonitor Publications, 18 Doughty Street, London WC1. This is an annual handbook.

An increasingly important role is now being played by the Statistical Office of the European Communities. Among their major reports are:

The General Statistical Bulletin
Bulletin of the European Communities
Economic Survey of Europe

Although these overviews or compilations can play an invaluable role in building up a picture of markets, the bulk of *actionable* data is constructed around specific markets.

Marketing in Europe is one of a number of invaluable publications issued by the Economist Intelligence Unit, 27 St James's Place, London SW1.

Market Data Reports on European Industries consists of specific industry studies, published by Marketing Studies International, City Road, London EC1.

Published Data on European Industrial Markets, Industrial Aids Ltd, 14 Buckingham Palace Road, London SW1.

Directors Guide to the EEC, Institute of Directors, 16 Pall Mall, London SW1Y 5ED.

Non-European information sources

These vary enormously in quality and availability. Data on the United States is outstanding in its diversity, range and general standard. As in Britain, the *Statistical Abstract of the United States* provides a superb overview of the main features of economic life.

In many third world and socialist economies, the best source of commercially useful information lies in the *National Plan.* Any small businessman seeking to build up his trade in these countries should seek to study these documents.

In many parts of the world, economic groups and Customs Unions are playing an increasingly important role in the gathering and organization of statistical data on their region. These include the Council for Mutual Economic Assistance (sometimes called ComeCon), The Caribbean Community and Common Market (CARICOM), The Latin American Free Trade Area (LAFTA) and The Association of South East Asia Nations (ASEAN).

For the majority of British firms, specific intelligence on UK markets is the key to the effective use of market information.

Retail Business, monthly, Economist Intelligence Unit. This concentrates on consumer products distributed through retailers.

Retail Intelligence, quarterly, Mintel, 20 Buckingham Street, The Strand, London, WC2.

Mintel, monthly, Mintel (as above). This covers a wide range of consumer products regularly.

Key Notes, Key Note Publications, 28–42 Banner Street, London EC1. These are a series of detailed descriptions of the key characteristics of a very large number of markets/industries.

Business Monitors, HMSO. These provide summaries of the statistical data on specific industry sectors.

This information can be supplemented by a wide range of magazines and periodicals relating to particular trades, industries and professions. These can be identified through *Benn's Press Directory*, Benn Publications, Sovereign Way, Tonbridge, Kent. A great deal of further material can be obtained from Trade Associations, Industry Research Associations and Industry Training Boards. The vast majority of these can be identified in the *Directory of British Associations*, CBD Publications, mentioned earlier.

Although these publications provide pictures of specific markets, information on specific firms or organizations may be necessary for some purposes. Here a number of publications are very useful.

Company Accounts often provide an excellent overview of the company, while giving some clues to its preoccupations and objectives.

A number of firms and publications exist to organize and collate this type of individual firm or product information, including:

The Centre for Interfirm Comparisons, West Stockwell Street, Colchester, Essex. The Centre provides information which firms can use to compare their performance with others.

Credit Ratings Ltd, City Road, London EC1, supply company profile and performance data.

Dunn and Bradstreet Ltd, 26/32 Clifton Street, London EC2, publish a wide range of useful reference texts, *Key British Enterprises, Stubbs Directory* and *Principal International Businesses.*

Extel, 37/45 Paul Street, London EC2, offer a range of services including *Handbook of Market Leaders, Extel Quote Service* (information on quoted firms) and *Extel Unquoted Service.*

ICC Business Ratios, 23 City Road, London EC1, sell a large number of reports on sectors of British business.

Jordan's Business Information Service, Jordan House, 47 Brunswick Place, London N1, supply detailed information on a large number of UK firms.

Kelly's Directories, IPC Business Press, 40 Bowling Green Lane, London EC1, publish a range of directories including *Kelly's Manufacturers and Merchants Directory, Kelly's Regional Directory of British Industry, Kelly's Post Office London Directory.*

Kompass Directories, Windsor Court, East Grinstead House, East Grinstead, West Sussex RH19 1ZB. These cover Australia, Belgium, Brazil, Denmark, France, Holland, Indonesia, Italy, Morocco, Norway, Singapore, Spain, Sweden, Switzerland and West Germany, as well as the UK.

The Retail Directory, Newman, Portland Street, London W1, provides information on British retailers.

Sells Directory, Sells Publications Ltd, Sells House, East Street, Epsom, Surrey, gives an alphabetical listing of 65,000 firms.

Standard and Poor's Register of Corporations, Directors and Executives, provides information on almost 40,000 US firms.

Stores of the World Directory gives a listing of major stores world-wide.

Thomas's Register of American Manufacturers is by far the most comprehensive listing of firms and industries in the USA.

Access

No small firm could afford to purchase or subscribe to the vast array of data sources listed above. However, Britain's excellent and accessible library network provides an invaluable resource.

Central and Local Libraries   Most cities and towns can boast good libraries, many have specialized commercial libraries with staff specially trained to assist with business enquiries. A major source of information held by many is extensive collections of *Yellow Pages* for Britain, Europe and North America. These can be very useful, especially in planning sales trips.

In most cases, the key to successful use of a library lies in effectively working with library staff.

Specialist Libraries

British Institute of Management Library, Management House, Parker Street, London.

Business Statistics Library, Cardiff Road, Newport, Gwent.

City Business Library, Gillett House, Basinghall Street, London EC2.

Science Reference Library, Business Information Service, British Library,

Southampton Buildings, Chancery Lane, London WC2.
Statistics and Marketing Intelligence Library, 1 Victoria Street, London SW1.

Besides these, many Chambers of Commerce have libraries or access to specialist library facilities.

New technologies

The growth of new information technologies is already having a major impact on the provision of marketing information. Telecommunications based 'Viewdata' systems such as *Prestel* can provide immediate access to a vast data base. The *Prestel Directory* lists the various types and form of material available. Computer data bases are growing in importance, particularly for highly specialized information search. The two most commonly available are *The Lockhead Data Base* (largely US information) and *Euronet* (European information).

Organizations

As mentioned above, a number of specialist organizations have emerged which can provide marketing information or specialist advice. These include:

Advertising Association, 15 Wilton Road, London SW1V 1NJ.
Advertising Standards Authority, 15–17 Ridgemont Street, London WC1E 7AW.
British Overseas Trade Board, 1 Victoria Street, London SW1 (and regional offices).
British Technology Group, 12–18 Grosvenor Gardens, London SW1.
Central Statistical Office, Great George Street, London SW1.
Cosira – see local offices in telephone directory.
Department of Industry, 1 Victoria Street, London SW1 (and regional offices).
Distributive Industries Sector Working Party, Millbank Tower, London SW1.
Industrial Market Research Society, Bird Street, Lichfield, Staffordshire.
The Institute of Marketing, Moor Hall, Cookham, Maidenhead (note, in particular, Marketing Advisory Service).
Institute of Export, World Trade Centre, London E1 1AA.
Institute of Physical Distribution Management, Management House, Parker Street, London WC2B 5PT.

Institute of Practitioners in Advertising, 44 Belgrave Square, London SW1X 8QS.

Institute of Public Relations, 1 Great James Street, London WC1.

Institute of Purchasing and Supply, Easton House, Easton-on-the-Hill, Stamford, Lincolnshire PE9 3NZ.

Local Enterprise Development Unit, Lamont House, Purdys Lane, Mewtownbreda, Belfast.

Market Research Society, 15 Belgrave Square, London SW1A 8PF.

Scottish Development Agency, Telford Road, Edinburgh.

Index

234

Starting the business was your first problem. Here's how to keep it *going* and *growing*.

The key to keeping your business going is to keep it growing. That means you need more people to help you, bigger premises, more customers and maybe even new products. And as your company grows, your accounts get more complex and less understandable. Suddenly your small business isn't so small any more, and it's hard to keep control.

The only way to cope is to call in the experts. The new *Building Your Business* series is a unique collection of tips and techniques from top business consultants who have already experienced *and solved* the problems you're facing now. Each book is packed with practical business know-how to help *you* keep *your* business going and growing.

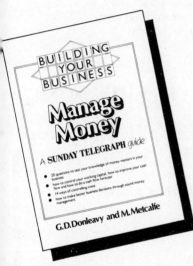

* how to answer your bank manager's questions
* 14 ways to control your costs
* how to do a cash flow forecast
* how good money management helps you make better business decisions

* how to get the best out of people *and* keep them happy
* checklists for improving performance, setting targets and writing job descriptions
* how to be a better negotiator — both with your employees and your customers

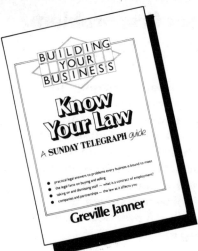

* practical legal answers to problems every business is bound to meet
* the legal facts on buying and selling
* taking on and dismissing staff — what is a contract of employment?
* companies and partnerships — the law as it affects you

Building Your Business books are available from your local bookseller. You can also order copies direct from Business Books, using the form below.

BUILDING
YOUR
BUSINESS